BOOST YOUR

VOCABULARY 2

Chris Barker

PENGUIN ENGLISH GUIDES

Pearson Education Limited
Edinburgh Gate
Harlow
Essex CM20 2JE, England
and Associated Companies throughout the world.

ISBN 0 582 46878 7

First published 2001
Copyright © Chris Barker 2001
Second impression 2004

Design and typesetting by Mackerel Creative Services
Illustrations by Mark Davis
Printed in China/ SWTC/02

Acknowledgements

With thanks to Helen Parker of Penguin Longman Publishing, for helping to shape the material and for her encouragement during the writing process; to Theresa Clementson, whose good sense, good humour and hard work made the transition from typescript to printed page seem effortless; and to Diane Winkleby, who opened my eyes to some of the delights of American English.

Chris Barker
London, 2001

The publishers make grateful acknowledgement for permission to reproduce the following photographs:
p 6, Denise Lewis, © All Sport; p 6, Ricky Martin, All Star Picture Library; p 9, copy of Michelangelo's 'David', © Art Archive/Album/Joseph Martin; p 10, Pete Sampras, © Gary M Prior/All Sport; p 10, Leonardo DiCaprio, © Ed Geller/Retna ; p 10, Venus Williams, © Daniel Moloshok/All Sport; p 10, Britney Spears, © Rex; p 10, David Coulthard, © Clive Mason/All Sport; p 28 Charlie's Angels, © Doc/MPA/Retna; p 40, *Secrets and Lies*, © CIBY 2000, courtesy of Kobal Collection; *Titanic*, © 20th Century Fox/Paramount, courtesy of Kobal Collection; *Red Corner*, © MGM, courtesy of Kobal Collection; *Wallace and Gromit*, © Rex; *Before Sunrise*, © Castle Rock/Detour, courtesy of Kobal Collection; *Red Planet*, © Mars Productions/Village Roadshow, courtesy of Kobal Collection; *The Simpsons*, © Retna; *Gladiator*, © Dreamworks/Universal, courtesy of Kobal Collection; *Reservoir Dogs*, © Live Entertainment, courtesy of Kobal Collection; *Frankenstein*, © Universal, courtesy of Kobal Collection; *Pale Rider*, © Warner Bros, courtesy of Kobal Collection; *Thelma and Louise,* © MGM/Pathe, courtesy of Kobal Collection; *Mr Bean*, © Polygram, courtesy of Kobal Collection; *Evita*, © Cinergi Pictures, courtesy of Kobal Collection; p 41, *Billy Elliot*, © Rex; p 66, lady with glasses, © Digital Vision Ltd

Published by Pearson Education Limited in association with Penguin Books Ltd, both companies being subsidiaries of Pearson plc.

For a complete list of the titles available from Penguin English please write to your local Pearson Education office or to: Penguin Englisht Marketing Department, Pearson Education, Edinburgh Gare, Harlow Essex CM20 2JE.

Contents

Introduction

Finding the right words

How many times do we want to say something in another language but we can't find the words?

Learning a language means that you start with a few words and phrases and slowly add to them. It is hardest in the early stages, because there's so much you want to say and you only have a small number of words. This is why it is important to try to increase your vocabulary as quickly as possible.

You will find that some words and phrases are more useful to you than others. You need to focus on these and try to learn them so you can use them. You don't have to learn every word or phrase.

Topics, words and phrases

In this book, we have chosen the topics which you often cover at the elementary level of an English course (see the previous page for the list of contents). Under each topic, you will find important ('key') words and phrases. If you use these words and phrases frequently, you will be able to remember them better. The exercises under each topic usually start with single words, making sure you can spell them correctly, and build towards longer writing activities.

How to use *Boost Your Vocabulary 2*

You can use this book on your own, for self-study, or in a class with your teacher. It can be used in three ways:

1 **To practise and learn more vocabulary**

- Choose a topic area of interest to you.

- Read the lists of words and phrases in the topic area.

- Translate the words and phrases into your language in the spaces provided, using a good bilingual dictionary.

- Do the practice exercises. Try not to refer to the lists when you are writing.

- Check your work by looking back at the lists.

- Finally, use the Answer key to mark and correct your work.

2 **To help you with written and spoken work**

When you are working on a particular topic in class, use the lists to help you with writing or speaking.

Do the practice exercises at home to help you use the words and phrases in a variety of contexts.

3 **To revise before a test**

Test yourself on particular topics by looking at your translations and saying the English words or phrases.

Try this on your own and with a partner.

Types of exercise

There are word puzzles, quizzes, surveys and questionnaires; there are exercises which ask you to organize words into groups; and there are opportunities for continuous writing. They aim to help you remember vocabulary and use it correctly.

Symbols

Some of the exercises have symbols, to help you identify them quickly:

 spelling

 word groups

 memorization

 When you see this symbol, you should write in your notebook.

 You will also find some words and phrases in a green box with this symbol. These focus on grammatical aspects.

Answer key

You can find the answers to the exercises and the tests in the centre of the book, in a special pull-out section.

Tests

There are tests after Units 4, 8 and 12. They revise the language of Units 1 to 4, 5 to 8 and 9 to 12. They will help you to see how well you are doing.

Self assessment and progress checks

On page 88 you will find charts which will help you to assess and record how much progress you are making.

Reference

REF When you see this symbol, you can find more information in the reference section at the back of the book. The reference section also contains some basic spelling rules, which follow on from those in *Boost Your Vocabulary 1*. It includes British and American spelling differences (*colour* and *color*, for example) and a unit-by-unit list comparing British and American English vocabulary.

1 Physical description

Translate the words and phrases.

The body

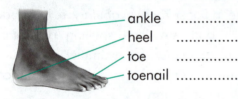

.... head   neck ....

.... shoulder   chest ....

.... arm   back ....

.... elbow   stomach ....

.... hand   waist ....

.... leg   hips ....

.... thigh   bottom ....

.... knee   foot (feet) ....

The foot

ankle ....

heel ....

toe ....

toenail ....

The hand

nail ....

finger ....

thumb ....

wrist ....

The head

hair ....   forehead ....

eye ....   eyebrow ....

nose ....   eyelashes ....

ear ....   lip ....

cheek ....   tongue ....

tooth (teeth) ....   mouth ....

chin ....

Skin

(He's)		(She's got)	
pale	....	freckles	....
fair-skinned	....	spots	....
dark	....	a scar	....
tanned	....	a mole	....

Features of the face

a /	round	face	....	dark brown	eyes	....
an	square		....	light blue		....
	long, thin		....	hazel		....
	oval		....	greenish brown		....
	small	nose	....	long	eyelashes	....
	big		....	thick		....
	long		....	strong features		....
	straight		....	high cheekbones		....

He wears glasses.   ....
He's got a beard.   ....
He's got a moustache.   ....

Hair style

long	....	(I've got)	
short	....	a centre parting.	....
medium-length	....	a side parting.	....
straight	....	long, straight hair.	....
curly	....	medium-length, wavy hair.	....
wavy	....		
frizzy	....	I wear my hair ...	....
spiky	....	in bunches.	....
cropped	....	in a pony tail.	....
(I've got)		in plaits.	....
a fringe.	....	in dreadlocks.	....
a shaved head.	....	tied back.	....
		up.	....

Hair type

thick	....
fine	....
dry	....
greasy	....
balding	....
bald	....

I've got thick hair.

....

He's going bald.

....

My hair sometimes gets greasy.

....

Listen, Tracy, spots are quite normal for people of our age. Just don't worry about them.

REF   *See page 86 for the British / American word list.*

1

 1a Circle the words in the wordsnake. The last letter of one word is the first letter of the next.

(c h i n)o s e y e l b o w a i s t h u m b a c k n e e y e b r o w r i s t h i g h i p s

1b Now circle twenty parts of the body in the wordsearch.

W	S	T	O	M	A	C	H	E	N
C	H	I	N	H	A	I	R	Y	O
F	O	R	E	H	E	A	D	E	S
I	U	T	N	M	A	N	K	L	E
N	L	O	A	O	R	K	J	A	N
G	D	N	I	U	B	L	P	S	E
E	E	G	L	T	O	O	T	H	C
R	R	U	C	H	E	E	K	E	K
T	O	E	D	M	C	H	E	S	T
L	I	P	B	O	T	T	O	M	R

2 Put the words in exercises 1a and 1b into the correct categories.

The head
forehead ....
chin ....
....
....
....
....
....

The body
....
....
....
....
....
....
....
....

THE BODY

The leg and the foot
....
....
....
....
....

The arm and the hand
....
....
....
....
....

3 Complete the description of this exercise.

SO YOU WANT A PERFECT BODY?
OK, start exercising!

Exercise 1

1  Lie on your b _a c k_ and put both your h _ _ _ _ up by the sides of your h _ _ _ (or across your c _ _ _ _ if you are new to this exercise).

2  Bend your k _ _ _ _ up. Keep them and your a _ _ _ _ _ together and keep your b _ _ _ _ _ on the floor.

3  Move your k _ _ _ _ to one side so that they make a 45° angle to the floor.

4 Move your upper body forwards, towards your l _ _ _ , then back again. Keep your s _ _ _ _ _ _ _ _ relaxed.

5 Repeat fifteen to twenty times.

4 Tracy and Wayne have tried a lot of hairstyles. Describe them using the words in the box.

| cropped | wavy | fringe | frizzy | dreadlocks |
| straight | curly | bunches | pony tail | spiky |

Wayne

Tracy

1 *Wayne's got wavy hair.* ....

2 *He's wearing his hair in a pony tail.* ....

3 ....

4 ....

5 ....

6 ....

7 ....

8 ....

9 ....

10 ....

1

5a How would you describe these people? Underline the correct words.

Pete Sampras has got a round / an oval face and thin / thick eyebrows. He's dark / fair-skinned. His hair is spiky / curly.

Leonardo DiCaprio's got a square / an oval face. He's dark / fair-skinned. He's got very big / quite small eyes and a small / big nose. He's got fine / thick hair, and it's short / long.

Venus Williams has got an oval / a round face. She's got wavy / curly hair, which she wears tied back / up.

5b Now write similar descriptions of the singer Britney Spears and the racing driver David Coulthard.

....
....
....
....

....
....
....
....

6 Complete the form to describe yourself.

On File Model Agency

Application form
Please complete this questionnaire about yourself and send it with your photos.

I'm ☐ pale ☐ fair-skinned
☐ dark ☐ tanned

I've got ☐ freckles ☐ spots
☐ a scar ☐ a mole / moles

My skin's quite dry ☐
I've got good skin ☐
I sometimes get spots ☐
I never get spots ☐

I've got .... eyes.

I've got ☐ long hair ☐ short hair
☐ medium-length hair ☐ cropped hair
☐ straight hair ☐ curly hair
☐ wavy hair ☐ frizzy hair
☐ a fringe ☐ a shaved head
☐ thick hair ☐ fine hair
☐ a centre parting ☐ a side parting
☐ dry hair ☐ greasy hair

I sometimes wear my hair
☐ up ☐ tied back
☐ in a pony tail ☐ in bunches
☐ in dreadlocks ☐ in plaits

7 Now write a description of your brother, sister or best friend using the phrases in exercise 6.

My best friend Becky is fair-skinned.
....
....
....

8 Write ten words and five expressions you are going to memorize.

Words		Expressions	
1	....	1	....
2	....		....
3	....	2	....
4	....		....
5	....	3	....
6	....		....
7	....	4	....
8	....		....
9	....	5	....
10	....		....

2 House and home

Translate the words and phrases.

The kitchen

cupboard ....
shelf (shelves) ....
cooker ....
oven ....
hob ....
microwave ....
dishwasher ....
washing machine ....
fridge ....
freezer ....
sink ....
taps ....
handle ....
drawers ....
wastebin ....
work surface ....
coffee machine ....
kettle ....
teapot ....
toaster ....
blinds ....

The living room

sofa ....
television / TV ....
armchair ....
coffee table ....
floorboards ....
rug ....
sound system ....
stool ....
table lamp ....
standard lamp ....
bookcase ....
bookshelf ....
picture ....
vase ....
curtains ....
radiator ....
fireplace ....
mantelpiece ....

light bulb ....
socket
cable ....
plug ....

The bedroom

double bed ....
single bed ....
bunk beds ....
plain / patterned
  carpet ....
chest of drawers ....
computer ....
desk ....
desk lamp ....
dressing table ....
duvet ....
notice board ....
radio alarm ....
wardrobe ....
wastepaper bin ....

The bathroom

bath ....
shower ....
toilet ....
toilet roll ....
soap dish ....
towel rail ....
washbasin ....
mirror ....
linen basket ....
bath towel ....
hand towel ....
flannel ....
toothbrush ....

Types of house

detached house

....

semi-detached house

....

terraced house

....

bungalow

....

cottage

....

farmhouse

....

flat

....

Abbreviations

Rd   Road   ....
St   Street   ....
Ave Avenue   ....

Where do you live?

....

In north London.

....

Wherabouts exactly?

....

In Camden Town. Our flat is above a shop
in Park Street.

....

What's it like there?

....

It's quite noisy.

....

I live at 45 Westcliff Road.

....

It takes about fifteen minutes to get to the
centre of town by bus.

....

🔍 Location

in the country ....

in a town / village ....

in + *name of street* ....

in + *name of town /
  village / area* ....

in a suburb called ....

in a quiet /
  busy street ....

in the mountains ....

near the sea ....

near the city centre ....

a long way from
  the city centre ....

**about twenty
  minutes' walk
  from** the city centre ....

**on the outskirts
  of** town ....

quite close to a
  park ....

above a shop ....

next to a café ....

opposite the
  post office ....

What are your neighbours like?

I don't know, really.
You never hear them.

REF   *See page 86 for the British / American
      word list.*

2

 1 Put the items in the room where you normally find them. Some items can go in several rooms, but just choose one.

washbasin	bath	duvet	microwave
fireplace	fridge	radio alarm	wardrobe
sink	sofa	television	freezer
toothbrush	oven	flannel	vase

kitchen

living room

HOUSE / FLAT

bathroom

washbasin

bedroom

 2a Match the two parts of these words (1k *coffee table*). Then add them to the correct room in exercise 1.

1	coffee	a)	basket
2	double	b)	surface
3	towel	c)	bin
4	toilet	d)	drawers
5	bath	e)	dish
6	chest of	f)	lamp
7	linen	g)	machine
8	soap	h)	rail
9	sound	i)	roll
10	standard	j)	bed
11	washing	k)	table
12	wastepaper	l)	system
13	work	m)	bulb
14	light	n)	towel

2b Find ten things in the picture from exercises 1 and 2a. Write the words below.

1 *bath towel* ....   6 ....

2 ....   7 ....

3 ....   8 ....

4 ....   9 ....

5 ....   10 ....

abc ✓ **3** Solve the crossword.

	D¹	R	A²	W	E	R	S			³	
								⁴			
⁵											
						⁶					
				⁷			⁸				
⁹											
			¹⁰							¹¹	
¹²		¹³									
						¹⁴					
¹⁵											

Across ▶

1 A chest of ...... (7)
4 Turn this on to get some water. (3)
5 Do you prefer a bath or a ......? (6)
7 An oven + a hob = a ...... (6)
9 I live ...... 45 Park Road. (2)
10 You toast bread in a .... (7)
12 The cold water's OK, but there's no ...... water. (3)
14 It goes into an electrical socket. (4)
15 Rd. (4)

Down ▼

1 No more washing-up! We've got a .... (10)
2 We live in a flat ...... a shop. (5)
3 It's got four legs, and it's the name of a mountain in South Africa. (5)
6 Our house is next ...... a field. (2)
7 I live quite ...... to the sports centre. (5)
8 You boil water in it. (6)
11 A small carpet. (3)
13 You make this favourite English drink in a ......pot. (3)

4 Look carefully at these two pictures and find four more differences.

Picture 1

There are two armchairs.
....
....
....
....
....

Picture 2

There's only one armchair.
....
....
....
....
....

 5 Describe the living room and the kitchen in your house or flat.

6 Match each description to a picture. Complete the descriptions by choosing from these words.

in	near	opposite	next	above	on

a

1 I live ....*in*............. Cornwall, ... the sea. Our house is called 'Penhaven'. It's a detached house. It isn't .... a village. The nearest town is Padstow.

Picture ...

b

2 I live .... London, ... a suburb called Hounslow. It's a long way from the centre of London. It's .... Heathrow Airport. I live .... a terraced house .... a busy street, but it is .... to a park.

Picture ...

c

GENERAL STORE

3 I live .... the country, ... a village called Elterwater, which is .... the Lake District. Our cottage is .... the post office.

Picture ...

d

4 I live .... Aviemore in Scotland. It's .... the mountains. It takes about half an hour to get to the nearest big town, Inverness.

Picture ...

e

PAYNE & SONS LIMITED

5 I live .... Ilkley, a town .... North Yorkshire. Our flat is .... a shop, ... the outskirts of town. It's .... Ripley Road. It's quite close to my school.

Picture ...

7 Write an account of where Amy lives.

Amy lives ....
....
....
....
....

 8 Write an account of where you live. Use these notes to help you.

City / Town	Country	Other	Area	Type
outskirts	small town	sea	busy / quiet	house
centre	village	mountains	near…	flat
suburb		nearest city		farm

 9 Write ten words and five expressions you are going to memorize.

Words		Expressions	
1	....	1	....
2	....		....
3	....	2	....
4	....		....
5	....	3	....
6	....		....
7	....	4	....
8	....		....
9	....	5	....
10	....		....

3 Eating in and eating out

Translate the words and phrases.

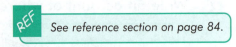 *See reference section on page 84.*

Quantities

litre ....
pint ....
100 g (grams) ....
kilo ....
100 ml (millilitres) ....
piece ....
bar ....
loaf (of bread) ....
slice *(noun)* ....
teaspoonful ....
small amount ....
a little ....

Containers

packet ....
tub ....
jar ....
carton ....
bottle ....
can ....
tin ....

Table items

knife (knives) ....
fork ....
soup spoon ....
dessert spoon ....
teaspoon ....
bowl ....
plate ....
side plate ....
glass ....
cup ....
saucer ....
jug ....
coffee pot ....
table mat ....
napkin ....

Preparing food (verbs)

chop ....
slice ....
grate ....
peel ....
mix ....
add ....
pour ....

Cooking food (verbs)

boil ....
fry ....
bake ....
roast ....
grill ....
poach ....
steam ....
heat ....

You can use the verbs above to make adjectives.
Popular British dishes

boiled carrots   mashed potatoes
grated carrots   scrambled eggs
fried fish   **but**
baked potatoes   roast chicken
grilled sausages   roast potatoes

Places to eat and drink

restaurant ....
café ....
fast-food restaurant...............................
pizzeria ....
sandwich bar ....
takeaway ....
pub ....

In a restaurant

menu	....
starter	....
main course	....
dessert	....

MUNCH MUNCH

I hate school dinners.

So do I.

Describing food

salty	....
sweet	....
tender	....
overcooked	....
underdone	....
raw	....
just right	....
fresh	....
spicy	....
burnt	....
tasty	....
delicious	....
nice	....
disgusting	....
horrible	....

Modifying expressions

not very	a bit	rather	very / really	too

(My roast chicken's) not very tasty. ....

(My toast is) a bit burnt. ....

(This curry's) rather spicy. ....

(Mm, my roast potatoes are) really nice. ....

(These french fries are) too salty. ....

Asking for a table and ordering a meal

You
Could I have a table for four, please? ....

To start, I'd like... ....

As a main course, I'll have... ....

Could I have some more bread, please? ....

Could I have the bill, please? ....

Waiter
What would you like? ....

What can I get you? ....

Anything to drink? ....

Enjoy your meal! ....

The chicken is served with rice. ....

REF See page 86 for the British / American word list.

1 Label the table items.

1 *napkin* ....

2 ....

3 ....

4 ....

5 ....

6 ....

7 ....

8 ....

9 ....

10 ....

11 ....

12 ....

2a Try out your cooking skills!

Do you know how to make a pancake?

Add the quantities in the box to the ingredients.

Ingredients

a little .... lemon juice .... of milk

.... of flour .... of oil

.... egg .... sugar

a little	a small amount
125g	a teaspoonful of
300 ml	one

Complete the instructions and put them in the right order.

Method

..1.. *Mix* .... the flour with the milk.

.... a little of the mixture into the pan.

...... Put it on a warm plate and .... it with lemon juice and sugar.

...... Then .... the egg.

.... the oil in a frying pan.

...... When the pancake's cooked on one side, flip it over.

mix	add	heat
pour	serve	

2b Write the list of ingredients and the method for your own favourite dish.

3 Put the words into the correct categories. Then next to each word write an appropriate item of food.

bake	chop	a carton	200g
boil	a bar	grate	grill
half a litre	a jar	a loaf	a packet
peel	roast	a tin	add

ways of cooking food

bake .... a cake ....

....

....

....

quantities

200g .... of butter ....

....

....

....

containers

a carton .... of milk ....

....

....

....

FOOD

ways of preparing food

chop .... an onion ....

....

....

....

4 Wayne and Tracy were really hungry and thirsty when they got to Tracy's house after school. Use the words in box A and the pictures in box B to write what they had.

A

1 slice   a slice of ham ....

2 bar   ....

3 can   ....

4 carton   ....

5 loaf   ....

6 bottle   ....

7 piece   ....

8 tub   ....

9 packet   ....

10 tin   ....

B

5 Look at the survey and complete the chart.

SURVEY
Fried, boiled or poached? British teenagers tell us how they like their food.

eggs
a) fried
b) boiled
c) poached

fish
a) fried
b) steamed
c) grilled

chicken
a) fried
b) grilled
c) roast

potatoes
a) boiled
b) chips
c) baked

carrots
a) boiled
b) steamed
c) raw

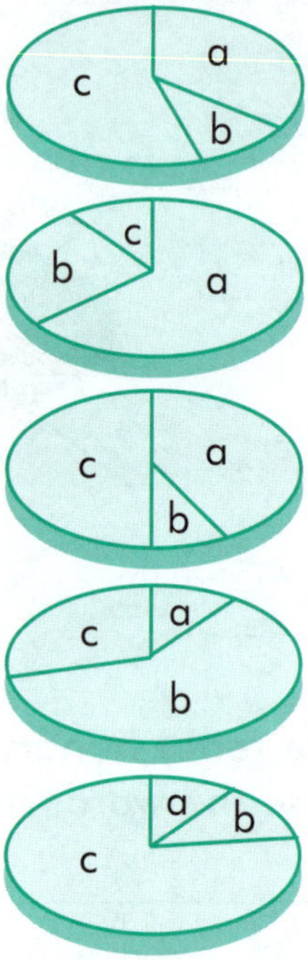

Results

Their favourite
poached eggs
....
....
....
....

My favourite
....
....
....
....
....

6a Write the descriptions in the correct column.

6b Choose different descriptions for 1 to 8.

rather spicy	too salty	delicious	too sweet
burnt	just right	underdone	very tender
very fresh	very tasty	overcooked	disgusting

Positive
....
....
....
....

Negative
rather spicy ....
....
....
....

1 toast   *burnt* ....
2 curry   ....
3 birthday cake ....
4 cooked vegetables ....
5 fish   ....
6 meat (e.g. a steak) ....
7 bread   ....
8 chips   ....

7a Match the menus to the places.

1 café c)...   3 fast food restaurant ......   5 Chinese takeaway ......
2 sandwich bar ...... 4 pizzeria ......   6 restaurant ......

7b Add your two favourite fillings to menu f.

7c Give examples of a starter, a main course and a dessert for menu b.

starter ....   main course ....   dessert ....

....

a) **Margherita** The original!
    Napoletana Very tasty!
    Calzone Inside there's ham, cheese and tomato … mmm, delicious!

f) **Top five fillings**
    1 tuna with salad and mayonnaise
    2 chicken with salad
    3 cheese and tomato
    4 ....
    ....
    5 ....
    ....

b) **Pre-theatre menu**
    3 courses, with wine, £17.50

c) Espresso
    Cappuccino

d) Hamburger and French fries £1.79
    Cheeseburger and French fries £1.99

e) All dishes served with special fried rice
    or
    steamed noodles

8 Write ten words and five expressions you are going to memorize.

Words		Expressions	
1	....	1	....
2	....		....
3	....	2	....
4	....		....
5	....	3	....
6	....		....
7	....	4	....
8	....		....
9	....	5	....
10	....		....

4 Places in towns

Translate the words and phrases.

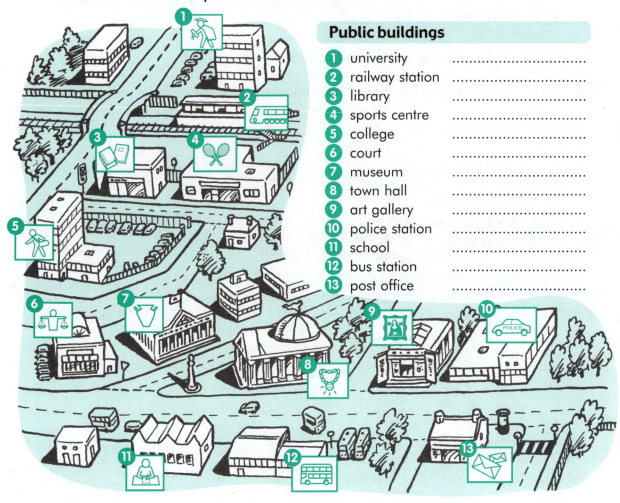

Public buildings

1 university ....
2 railway station ....
3 library ....
4 sports centre ....
5 college ....
6 court ....
7 museum ....
8 town hall ....
9 art gallery ....
10 police station ....
11 school ....
12 bus station ....
13 post office ....

Entertainment

cinema ....
theatre ....
concert hall ....
games arcade ....
bowling alley ....
skating rink ....
club ....
disco ....

Services

bank ....
bureau de change ....
hotel ....
tourist information
 (office) ....
laundrette ....
doctor's surgery ....
optician's ....
dentist's ....
health centre ....
job centre ....
estate agent's ....

Shops and shopping

shopping centre	....	stationer's	....
department store	....	dry cleaner's	....
supermarket	....	off licence	....
butcher's	....	video shop	....
baker's / bakery	....	hairdresser's	....
jeweller's	....	record shop	....
florist's / flower shop	....	toy shop	....
bookshop	....	hardware store	....
greengrocer's	....	electrical goods store	....
fishmonger's	....	clothes shop	....
chemist's	....	corner shop	....
newsagent's	....	market	....

The clothes shop has got a sale on.

....

There are lots of bargains.

....

There's a ten per cent discount on everything.

....

A few items are half price.

....

Are there any discounts for students?

You

Can I have ...? ....
Have you got any ...? ....
I'm just looking, thanks. ....
Could you help me? I'm looking for ... .
I'll take one of those, please. ....
How much is it? ....
Can I pay by credit card / cheque? ....
Could I have a receipt, please? ....

Shop assistant

Can I help you? ....
If you need any help, just ask. ....
Are you being served? ....
It's on special offer. ....
Anything else? ....
Would you like a bag? ....
Here's your change. ....
Sign here, please. ....
Here / there you are. ....

REF
See page 86 for the British / American word list.

4

1 Match each picture to a shop. Then, for each type of shop, give the name of one in your town.

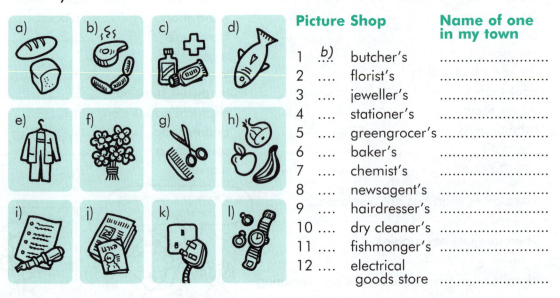

Picture	Shop	Name of one in my town
1 *b)*	butcher's	....
2	florist's	....
3	jeweller's	....
4	stationer's	....
5	greengrocer's	....
6	baker's	....
7	chemist's	....
8	newsagent's	....
9	hairdresser's	....
10	dry cleaner's	....
11	fishmonger's	....
12	electrical goods store	....

2a Match the words in the two columns. Some words in the second column can be used twice. Then write the full name under the correct picture.

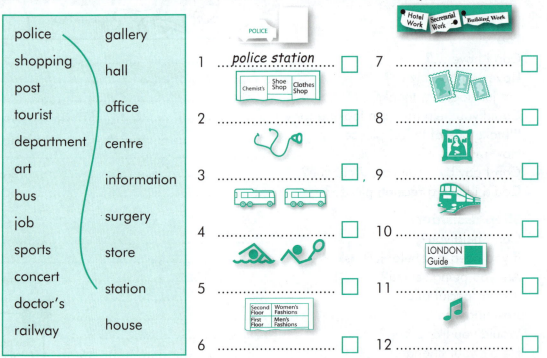

2b Tick the places that are within fifteen minutes' walk of your house or school.

3a Find fourteen more words for places in towns.

C	O	U	R	T	B	A	N	K	S
S	U	D	P	H	C	L	U	B	U
C	C	I	N	E	M	A	N	O	P
H	G	S	J	A	L	K	I	O	E
O	C	C	H	T	P	I	V	K	R
O	E	O	O	R	T	Y	E	S	M
L	V	H	T	E	D	N	R	H	A
M	U	S	E	U	M	P	S	O	R
C	O	L	L	E	G	E	I	P	K
L	A	U	N	D	R	E	T	T	E
S	L	I	B	R	A	R	Y	W	T

3b Put the words from the wordsearch in the correct group.

the law
.....court.....

education
....
....
....

culture and entertainment
....
....
....

shops
....
....

services
....
....

4 Where would you go?

1 You've got toothache. *I'd go to the dentist's.* ....

2 You've got a headache. ....

3 Your eyes hurt and you can't see the board at school. ....

4 You've got a lot of clothes to wash. ....

5 You've got a jacket which can't be washed. ....

6 You're looking for a flat to rent. ....

7 You've got to do the week's food shopping and you haven't got a lot of time. ....

8 You've seen an accident in the street. One of the cars drove away without stopping. ....

9 You're looking for a job. ....

10 You want to buy a new watch. ....

11 You're going to Australia on holiday and you want to change some money. ....

12 You want to buy some flowers for your friend's birthday. ....

4

5 Choose five of the following places in your town to take an English friend. Write sentences explaining your plans, giving details of each place.

concert hall	skating rink	bowling alley	cinema
theatre	games arcàde	club	disco

On Monday evening we'll go to a concert at the Barbican Concert Hall.
....

6 You are telephoning to book two tickets for *Charlie's Angels* this evening. Complete the dialogue.

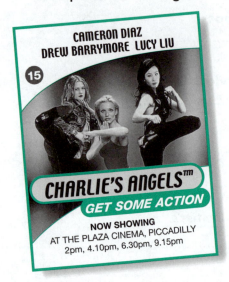

Assistant: Plaza Cinema, good afternoon.

You: *(say what you want)* .*I'd like*................
....

Assistant: Which performance?

You: *(decide and respond)* ....
....

Assistant: That'll be £15, please.

You: *(discount for students?)* ....
....

Assistant: Only for the two o'clock performance.

You: *(respond)* ....

Assistant: OK. That's fine. Could I have your credit card number?

7a Write 'S' for the shop assistant's sentences and 'C' for the customer's sentences in dialogues 1, 2 and 3.

7b Fill in the missing words.

7c Number the sentences in the correct order to make dialogues.

7d Write the type of shop in which each dialogue takes place.

Dialogue 1

S/C   **Correct order**

....   All washing machines come with a two-year guarantee. If you need any .*help*...................., just ask.

....   I will. Thank ....

....   Good morning. .... I help you?

....   I'm .... looking, thanks.

Type of shop   ....

Dialogue 2

S/C   **Correct order**

....   Yes, we have. It's just here.

....   Could I .... a receipt, please?

....   Are you .... served?

....   Yes, of course you can. Sign ...., please.

.... much is it?

....   It's £12.99. It's on .... offer.

....   No, I'm not. I'm .... for the latest Harry Potter book. Have you got it?

....   Of course. I'll .... it in the bag with the book.

....   Oh, that's good. It's £15 in other shops. I .... take it. Can I pay by credit ....?

Type of shop   ....

Dialogue 3

S/C   **Correct order**

....   I .... take a lettuce, please.

....   Good morning, Mrs Harris. What .... you like today?

....   Oh, yes. They came in this morning.

....   Anything ....?

....   There you .... A lettuce and some carrots. Two pounds, please.

....   Yes, some carrots, please. Are they fresh?

....   I've only got a £20 note. Have you got any ....?

....   In that case, I'll have a kilo.

Type of shop   ....

8   Write ten words and five expressions you are going to memorize.

Words		Expressions	
1	....	1	....
2	....		....
3	....	2	....
4	....		....
5	....	3	....
6	....		....
7	....	4	....
8	....		....
9	....	5	....
10	....		....

Test yourself 1 (Units 1 to 4)

How much can you remember?

My mark: _____
60

1 Label the picture.

0 *forehead* ....

1 e ....

2 n ....

3 t ....

4 l ....

5 c ....

6 h ....

7 e ....

8 c ....

9 m ....

10 n ....

(10 marks)

2 Complete the description of the girl in exercise 1.

Amy is 0 *fair-skinned*........ . She's got dark brown hair. It's 1 ....-length and she wears it in 2 .... She's got an 3 .... face. Around her nose, she's got 4 ....

(4 marks)

3 Solve the crossword.

Across ▶

1 This large store sells clothes, furniture, things for the kitchen, perfume and all sorts of things. (10)

5 It's in the wall, and it brings electricity into your home. (6)

7 Not cooked. (3)

8 If you want to buy a cooker or a fridge, go to an ... hardware store. (10)

10 ... the outskirts of town. (2)

11 I enjoyed that pasta dish. It was really ... . (5)

15 If you want to wake up early, use my ... - alarm. (5)

16 You've got a top one and a bottom one right under your nose! (3)

18 My hair sometimes ... greasy. (4)

19 Would you like a ... of water? (5)

1 D	E	2 P	A	R	T	3 M	E	N	4 T
5					6		7		
8				9					
				10					
11	12		13						14
					15				
	16	17							
18				19					

Down ▼

1 The sweet part of a meal. (7)

2 Two ... of crisps, please. (7)

3 I usually wear ... hair in a pony tail. (2)

4 You use it to dry yourself after a shower. (5)

6 ... the light on. (4)

7 I get all my CDs and cassettes from Andy's ... shop. (6)

9 If you want to buy presents for children, go to the ... shop in the High Street. (3)

12 I'm sorry I wasn't ... to come to your party. (4)

13 You turn them on to get water. (4)

14 They're at the end of your feet. (4)

15 It's made of cloth or wool and you put it on the floor. (3)

17 You live in that new block of flats. What's ... like there? (2)

(21 marks)

4 Complete the shopping list.

0	Two	*cartons*	of milk	4	A	of lemonade
1	A		of marmalade	5	A	of biscuits
2	A		of bread	6	A	of chocolate
3	Two		of tomatoes			

(6 marks)

5 Unscramble the words, which all start with the letter in dark type, and put them in the correct group.

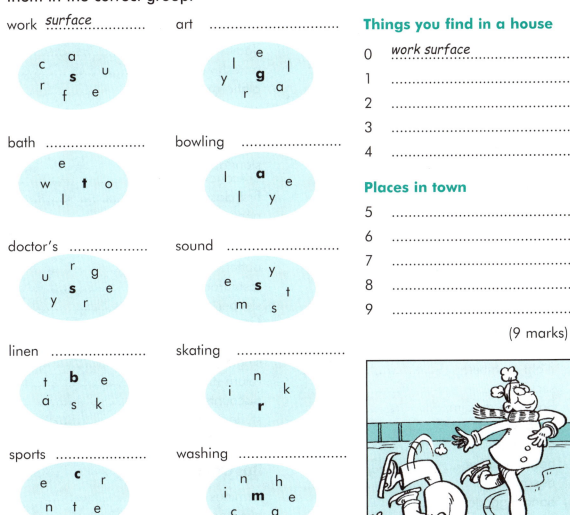

work *surface* ....

art ....

c a **s** u r f e

e l **g** l y r a

bath ....

bowling ....

e w **t** o l

l **a** e l y

doctor's ....

sound ....

r g u **s** e y r

y e **s** t m s

linen ....

skating ....

t **b** e a s k

n i k **r**

sports ....

washing ....

e **c** r n t e

n h i **m** e c a

Things you find in a house

0   *work surface* ....

1   ....

2   ....

3   ....

4   ....

Places in town

5   ....

6   ....

7   ....

8   ....

9   ....

(9 marks)

5 Travel and transport

Translate the words and phrases.

Vehicles

bus ....
coach ....
train ....
tram ....
plane ....
lorry ....
van ....
car ....
taxi / cab ....
motorbike ....
scooter ....
bike ....

> Use **by** with means of transport, e.g.
> by public transport, by bus, by coach,
> by train, etc.

Air travel

terminal ....
airline ....
arrivals ....
departures ....
departure lounge ....
check-in (desk) ....
passport control ....
gate ....
flight (number) ....
security ....
baggage reclaim ....
window seat ....
aisle seat ....
boarding pass ....
passport ....
hand luggage ....
first class ....
business class ....
economy class ....

Rail travel

terminus ....
arrivals ....
departures ....
information (desk) ....
waiting room ....
left-luggage
 (office / lockers) ....
ticket office ....
toilets:
 gentlemen / gents ....
 ladies ....
refreshments ....
platform ....
way out ....
timetable ....
direct train ....
standard class
 (second class) ....
first class ....
non-smoking
 compartment ....
no-smoking sign ....
buffet car ....
restaurant car ....
sleeper ....
fare ....
reservation ....
single (ticket) ....
return (ticket) ....
discounts ....
student card ....
rail card ....

Bus travel

terminus ....
bus stop ....
queue ....
bus pass ....
travel card ....
 (=rail and bus pass)

People

Train
ticket collector ....

driver ....

Bus
driver ....

conductor ....

Plane
pilot ....

cabin attendant ....

customs officer ....

immigration officer ....

Journeys

journey ....

trip ....

tour ....

on time ....

early ....

late ....

delayed ....

cancelled ....

REF See page 86 for the British / American word list.

Travelling (verbs)

leave ....

arrive ....

take (a train, bus,
    plane or taxi) ....

catch (a train, bus
    plane, but **not** a taxi) ....

miss (a train, bus or
    plane) ....

change (trains,
    buses, planes) ....

get on (a train,
    bus or plane) ....

get off (a train,
    bus or plane) ....

get out of (a car or taxi) ....

Plane travel
board ....

take off ....

land ....

And they say cycling keeps you fit.

HONK HONK

How much is the train fare? ....

Are there any discounts
    for students? ....

Is it cheaper if I book in advance? ....

Is there a train that leaves at
    about 7.30? ....

What time does the train get in? ....

Do I have to change? ....

Which platform is it? ....

Is this the train to …? ....

Train travel is …

| cheap / expensive ....

| quick / slow ....

| comfortable / uncomfortable ....

abc ✓ **1** You are at the railway station. What do these symbols mean?

1 *i* <u>i n f o r m a t i o n</u>

5 <u>w</u> _ _ <u>o</u> _ _

2 <u>t</u> _ _ _ _ _ <u>o</u> _ _ _ _ _

6 <u>r</u> _ <u>f</u> _ _ _ _ _ _ _ _

3 <u>n</u> _ <u>s</u> _ _ _ _ _

7 <u>b</u> _ _ _ _ and <u>t</u> _ _ _ _

4 <u>l</u> _ _ _ - <u>l</u> _ _ _ _ _   <u>l</u> _ _ _ _ _ <u>s</u>

8 <u>t</u> _ _ _ _ _ <u>s</u>

2 Choose the correct verb.

(get off /get out)
1 We're going to sit here all day in this taxi. The traffic is so bad.
Let's *get out* .... and walk.
2 The train stops at Didcot. You need to *get off* .... here.

(catch / take)
3 Hurry up, or you won't .... the train.
4 We decided to .... a taxi.

(get off / take off)
5 What time did their plane ....?
6 Ask the bus conductor to tell you where to ....

(get on / get in)
7 It's OK. There's enough room in the car. ....
8 I wanted to go to York but I .... the train to Leeds by mistake.

(land / get in)
9 What time did the train ....?
10 What time did the plane ....?

3 Write about a real or imaginary train journey, using the notes below.

Last summer I travelled from …

Journey from / to? ....

Class / single / return ticket? ....

Fare (student discount)? ....

Departure time (on time / late)? ....

Direct? ....

Refreshments? ....

Arrival time (early / late / on time)? ....

4 Write the words in the correct column. Some words can go in more than one column.

baggage reclaim	boarding pass	buffet car	cabin attendant
check-in desk	conductor	departure lounge	driver
return	immigration officer	left-luggage lockers	pass (*noun*)
pilot	passport	station	terminal
terminus	ticket collector	travel card	waiting room

	air travel	rail travel	bus travel
places and facilities	baggage reclaim		
people			
tickets and documents			

5 Complete the questionnaire.

DEPARTMENT OF TRANSPORT AND THE ENVIRONMENT
Please help us by filling in this questionnaire. Thank you.

In the past two weeks ...

1 ... which of the following means of transport have you used?

Bus ☐ Train ☐ Car ☐ Bike ☐
Other ☐ (please specify)

....

2 ... how much have you spent on

train tickets? ....
bus tickets? ....

3 ... approximately how many kilometres have you travelled

by public transport?.....................
by car? ....
by bike? ....

4 ... how many journeys have you made using the following means of transport?

• None   • 1 – 5   • More than 5

bike ....
public transport ....
car ....
taxi ....

5 In your opinion, what is the best way to travel? Why?

....
....
....
....

6 **Solve the crossword.**

Across ►

1 To find out when your train leaves, you need to look at the ...... board. (10)

5 With 7 Down. You can sit here before your train leaves. (7–4)

8 The plane took ...... on time. (3)

11 At your destination airport, you pick up your bags from the baggage ...... (7)

13 Two o'clock in the afternoon = 2 ...... (2)

14 The train leaves at 6.30. What time does it get ...... ? (2)

15 You look at them to find out train times. (10)

20 Passengers who would like dinner should go to the ...... car now. (10)

23 First ...... standard class? (2)

Down ▼

1 ...... I have to change? (2)

2 The train to Brighton leaves from 6. (8)

3 We went on a school ...... to France last year. (4)

4 There's a bus ...... right outside my house. (4)

6 The bus was full. I couldn't ...... on. (3)

7 See 5 Across.

9 Do you want a single or a return ...... ? (6)

10 A vehicle for transporting small objects. (3)

12 A measurement of distance equal to about 1.6 kilometres. (4)

15 They went on a ...... of the Greek islands. (4)

16 Hurry up! You don't want to ...... your train. (4)

17 You usually ...... the plane about twenty minutes before take off. (5)

18 Would you like a window or an aisle ...... ? (4)

19 I've got my driving licence, but I haven't got a .... (3)

21 Does this bus go ...... the town centre? (2)

22 You can't have a cigarette. There's a ...... smoking sign up there. (2)

The crossword grid contains the pre-filled letters: 1 Down **D O** (forming the start of a word), and 12 Down **M I L E**.

OUTWARD JOURNEY
NAME.........
DESTINATION ADDRESS.........
RESORT.........
STATION / A.........

Class	ticket type	Adult	Child
STD	TRAVELCARD	ONE	NIL
Date	Number	@1232494
26. JUN.1	32134	Price
From	Valid	£4.00
QUEENS PARK ROAD (LON)	Route
To	1746
A125* ZONES		TRAVELCARD

● **BETTER AIRWAYS**

7 Use the words in the box to complete the airport information leaflet.

airline	boarding pass	business	check in
control	departure	economy	first class
flight	gate	passport	hand luggage
security	terminal	ticket	

For your information

- Make sure you know which ..*terminal*........ your plane leaves from.

- When you arrive at the airport find the desks for your .... (e.g. British Airways, Air France).

- Make sure you are in the right queue. Your ticket will tell you which class you are travelling: ...., ... or ....

- The assistant at the desk will ask for your .... and your ....

- He or she will then .... your baggage and give you your ....

- Please note that you can only carry one item of .... onto the plane.

- You should then go through passport .... and through the .... check.

- Go to the .... lounge and check which .... your .... leaves from.

8 Write ten words and five expressions you are going to memorize.

Words	Expressions
1	1 ....
2	....
3	2 ....
4	....
5	3 ....
6	....
7	4 ....
8	....
9	5 ....
10	....

Cinema, television and radio

Translate the words and phrases.

Types of film

horror film	....	real-life drama	....
science fiction (sci-fi) film	....	thriller	....
		comedy	....
animated film	....	cartoon	....
historical film	....	epic	....
gangster movie	....	western	....
disaster movie	....	musical	....
road movie	....	love story	....

Talking about films and TV programmes

It's a blockbuster.   ....
It's a low-budget film.   ....
It's a classic.   ....
It's based on a book.   ....
It's subtitled.   ....
It's dubbed.   ....

It's beautifully filmed.   ....
It's quite moving.   ....
It's very funny.   ....
It's nonsense.   ....
The story is ridiculous.   ....

The acting is marvellous.   ....
She's superb in the title role. ....
He isn't very convincing.   ....

I like horror films.

That's because you can identify with the characters.

What's showing at the Roxy Cinema?   ....
When is the new *Star Wars* film coming out?   ....
Where's it on?   ....
Who's in it?   ....
Who's it directed by?   ....
What's it about?   ....
What time is *A question of sport* on?   ....
What channel is it on?   ....
It's on at 8.30 on BBC1.   ....
I missed last night's episode of *Friends*.   ....

Television and radio

music programme	....
travel programme	....
current affairs programme	....
arts programme	....
sports programme	....
wildlife programme	....
natural history programme	....
educational programme	....
talk show	....
chat show	....
quiz show	....
game show	....

series	....
comedy series	....
period drama	....
cartoon	....
soap (opera)	....
sitcom (situation comedy)	....
documentary	....
play	....
drama	....
news	....
regional news	....
weather forecast	....

.... remote
.... control

Turn the TV on / off.
....

Turn up / down the volume.
....

Fast-forward it.
....

Rewind it.
....

brightness	....
contrast	....
colour	....
channel	....

TV

Video

pause	....
play	....
stop	....
search	....

TV transmission

terrestrial	....
satellite	....
cable	....
digital	....

Radio

station	....
band	....
frequency	....
FM	....
AM	....

Give me the remote control!

REF *See page 87 for the British / American word list.*

1 Complete the words for types of film. Then match them with the pictures. Finally, give an example of each type of film (in English, if possible).

type of film	picture	example
1 a_nimat_ed_ film	d	
2 c _ m _ d _		
3 c _ _ t _ _ n		
4 g _ n _ s t _ _ film		
5 d _ s _ s t _ _ movie		
6 r _ _ l - l _ fe drama		
7 r _ _ d movie		
8 s c _ _ _ c _ - f _ c _ i _ n (s _ i - f _)		
9 w _ _ t _ _ n		
10 m _ s _ c _ l		
11 l _ v _ story		
12 h _ _ _ _ r film		
13 e p _ _		
14 t h _ _ l _ _ r		

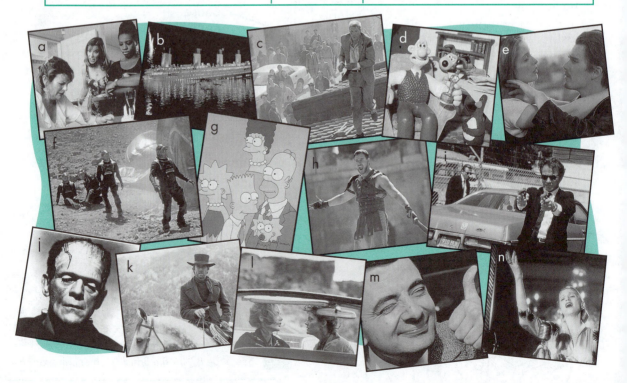

2 Decide whether the following descriptions are positive or negative.

	😊	☹			😊	☹
1 It's very funny.	✔		6 The story is ridiculous.			
2 It's quite moving.			7 The acting is awful.			
3 It's nonsense.			0 He isn't very convincing.			
4 It's a classic.			9 She's superb in the title role.			
5 It's beautifully filmed.			10 The animation is marvellous.			

3 Write a summary of a favourite film.

> Use a dictionary to help you write your summary, but keep it simple. Note that you can use the present simple for this type of description.

Name of film

What sort of film is it?

Who's it directed by?

(Is it based on a book?)

Who's in it?

What's it about?

What's the problem?

How does the film end?

What are the performances like?

Any other comments?

Rating: ★ to ★★★★★

Billy Elliot

Billy Elliot is part-comedy, part real-life drama. It's directed by Stephen Aldry.

It stars Jamie Bell as an 11-year-old who wants to be a ballet dancer. The problem is that his father and brother think ballet is silly. They want him to be a boxer. But Billy goes to dance lessons and finally achieves his dream.

Jamie Bell is superb in the title role. His dancing is totally convincing. The film is a classic.
★★★★★

4 Wayne and Tracy are watching a DVD. Complete what Wayne says.

1 The picture's quite dark.
   Turn up the brightness....................

2 I can't hear what they're saying.
   ....

3 There's something wrong with the picture. It's all black, white and grey.
   ....

4 I want to see that bit again!
   ....

5 I don't want to see the adverts. Let's go through them quickly.
   ....

6 I'm going to the toilet, but I don't want to miss anything.
   ....

5 Look at the programmes Wayne is going to watch this evening. Decide which type of programme each one is.

4.30	That Thing	A profile of American teenage singer, Britney Spears *music programme / documentary*
5.00	Learning Zone	Problems with Maths? Here are the answers
5.30	Oprah Winfrey	Members of the audience tell Oprah what they think
6.00	Hollyoaks	In this episode, things get serious when Ben tells Cindy he's got another girlfriend … and she's not happy
6.30	The Animal Zone	Giraffes in East Africa
7.30	Top of the Pops	Live bands, videos and the UK's number one single
8.00	The Colourists	Michael Palin presents a profile of four Scottish painters
9.00	Who Wants to be a Millionaire?	Answer the questions and win a big prize
9.30	Match of the Day	Finland v. England: highlights of today's game
10.30	Panorama	The war against drugs in Britain today

6 Look at the TV schedules for this week in a newspaper. Find an example of each type of programme, write its name and when it is on.

Type	Name of programme	When?
1 documentary	*The Hunger Business*	*It's on at 7.30pm on Friday. / There isn't one on this week.*
2 game show		
3 comedy series		
4 talk show		
5 drama		
6 natural history programme		

7 Try this quiz.

Quick quiz

🎬 Cinema

1 *Gladiator* is   a) an epic
                b) a western
                c) a sci-fi film
                              (1 mark)

2 *Mr Bean* is   a) a gangster movie
                b) a comedy
                c) a horror film
                              (1 mark)

3 A film which didn't cost a lot of money to make is called
         a) a blockbuster
         b) a low-budget film
         c) a soap
                              (1 mark)

4 A great film is sometimes called
         a) a thriller
         b) a documentary
         c) a classic
                              (1 mark)

🎵 Radio

5 **RADIO 1   FM   97.6–99.8 Mhz**
a) What is the frequency?
....
b) What is the name of the radio station?
....
c) What is the band?
....
                            (3 marks)

👁 TV

6 What do you call these kinds of TV transmission?
a) ....
b) ....
                            (2 marks)

7 *Tom and Jerry* and *The Simpsons* are popular ....
                            (1 mark)

Answers
Check your answers on page D.

How many questions did you answer correctly?
Marks out of 10

7–10   From Hollyoaks to Hollywood, you're hot!

4–6   Not bad
1–3   It's not your ambition to be a film star, is it?

8 Write ten words and five expressions you are going to memorize.

Words	Expressions
1	1 ....
2	....
3	2 ....
4	....
5	3 ....
6	....
7	4 ....
8	....
9	5 ....
10	....

Money

Translate the words and phrases.

English money

note	....
coin	....
pound	....
penny (pence)	....

> **English bank notes:** £50 (fifty pounds / a fifty-pound note), £20, £10 and £5.
>
> **English coins:** £2 (two pounds), £1, 50p (fifty p / fifty pence / a fifty-pence piece), 20p, 10p, 5p, 2p and 1p (a penny).

Banks

cashier	....
enquiries	....
travellers' cheques	....
current account	....
savings account	....
cheque book	....
paying-in book	....
ATM (automated telling machine) / cash machine	....

Foreign exchange till / Bureau de change

foreign currency	....
exchange rate	....
commission	....
How many pesetas are there to the pound?	

....

Cards

credit card	....
debit card	....
store card	....

Cheques

(name of who you are paying)

(amount in words)

account number

....

BANK OF WORLD COMMERCE 1, High Street, Leeds   65 65 42

Pay Mr. Jones and Co. Limited   May 1st

Forty-five pounds only   £ 45-00

A. Smith

0082746   12345678 00   A. Smith

branch

....

(amount in figures)

your signature

....

Shops

price	....
price tag	....
change	....
receipt	....
till / check-out	....
refund	....
exchange	....

Money and character

mean	....
generous	....
careful with money	....
careless with money	....

> *Change* is an uncountable noun, e.g. 'I'm sorry, I haven't got any change.' *Refund* and *exchange* are used as both verbs and nouns.

Answer key

1 Physical description

Exercise 1a

chin	back
nose	knee
eye	eyebrow
elbow	wrist
waist	thigh
thumb	hips

Exercise 1b

The head	The body
forehead	waist
chin	back
nose	hips
eye	stomach
eyebrow	chest
hair	bottom
tooth	neck
cheek	shoulder (could also go under
lip	'The arm and the hand')
tongue	
mouth	**The arm and the hand**
ear	elbow
eyelashes	thumb
	wrist
	finger
The leg and	nail (could also go under
the foot	'The leg and the foot')
thigh	
knee	
ankle	
toe	

Exercise 3

back	ankles
hands	bottom
head	knees
chest	legs
knees	shoulders

Exercise 4
Possible answers

1 *Wayne's got wavy hair.*
2 *He's wearing his hair in a pony tail.*
3 His hair is spiky.
4 He's wearing his hair in dreadlocks.
5 His hair is curly.
6 His hair is cropped.
7 Tracy's wearing her hair in bunches.
8 She's got straight hair.
9 Her hair is frizzy.
10 She's got a fringe.

Exercise 5a

Pete Sampras	Leonardo DiCaprio	Venus Williams
an oval	an oval	short
thick	fair-skinned	a round
dark	quite small	curly
curly	small	tied back
	thick	

Exercise 5b
Possible answers

Britney Spears has got an oval face. She's got big eyes and long eyelashes. She's got straight, medium-length hair.

David Coulthard's got a square face and a straight nose. He's got short, curly hair.

2 House and home

Exercise 1
Possible answers

kitchen	bathroom	living room	bedroom
sink	*washbasin*	fireplace	duvet
fridge	toothbrush	sofa	radio alarm
oven	bath	television	wardrobe
freezer	flannel	vase	
microwave			

Exercise 2a

		Possible answers
1	*coffee table*	living room
2j	double bed	bedroom
3h	towel rail	bathroom
4i	toilet roll	bathroom
5n	bath towel	bathroom
6d	chest of drawers	bedroom
7a	linen basket	bathroom
8e	soap dish	bathroom
9l	sound system	living room
10f	standard lamp	living room
11g	washing machine	kitchen
12c	wastepaper bin	bedroom
13b	work surface	kitchen
14m	light bulb	living room

Exercise 2b

1	*bath towel*	6	light bulb
2	washbasin	7	toothbrush
3	flannel	8	linen basket
4	bath	9	soap dish
5	towel rail	10	toilet roll

Exercise 3

Exercise 4

Picture 1

There are two armchairs.
There's a bookcase.
There's a lamp on the table.
There are floorboards.
There are blinds.

Picture 2

There's only one armchair.
There are bookshelves.
There's a vase of flowers on the table.
There's a carpet.
There are curtains.

Exercise 6

1 *in*	2 in /	3 in	4 in	5 in
near	near	in	near / in	in
in	in	near / in	Picture b	above
Picture d	in	near		on
	in / on	opposite		in / on
	next	Picture e		Picture c
	Picture a			

Exercise 7

Possible answer

Amy lives in a semi-detached house on West Street in Richmond. It's next to the Omega Café and it's a hundred metres from the river. It's quite near the airport.

3 Eating in and eating out

Exercise 1

1	*napkin*	7	glass
2	fork	8	jug
3	dinner plate	9	teaspoon
4	bowl	10	cup
5	knife	11	saucer
6	(soup) spoon	12	side plate

Exercise 2a

a little (lemon juice)	300ml (of milk)
125g (of flour)	a small amount (of oil)
one (egg)	a teaspoonful of (sugar)

1 *Mix (the flour with the milk).*
2 (Then) add (the egg).
3 Heat (the oil in a frying pan).
4 Pour (a little of the mixture into the pan).
5 (When the pancake's cooked on one side, flip it over.)
6 (Put it on a warm plate and) serve (it with lemon juice and sugar.

Exercise 3

Possible answers

ways of cooking food

bake	*a cake*
boil	potatoes
roast	a chicken
grill	a sausage

containers

a carton	*of milk*
a jar	of honey
a tin	of peaches
a packet	of biscuits

quantities

200g	*of butter*
half a litre	of milk
a bar	of chocolate
a loaf	of bread

ways of preparing food

chop	*an onion*
peel	an orange
grate	cheese
add	salt

Exercise 4

1 *a slice of ham*
2 a bar of chocolate
3 a can of cola / drink
4 a carton of orange juice
5 a loaf of bread
6 a bottle of lemonade
7 a piece of cheese
8 a tub of ice cream
9 a packet of sweets
10 a tin of soup

Exercise 5

poached eggs
fried fish
roast chicken
chips / potato chips
raw carrots

Exercise 6a

Positive	Negative
very fresh	*rather spicy*
just right	burnt
very tasty	too salty
delicious	underdone
very tender	overcooked
	too sweet
	disgusting

Exercise 6b

Possible answers

1 *burnt*
2 rather spicy / very tasty
3 delicious / too sweet
4 overcooked / just right
5 underdone / very fresh
6 very tender / just right
7 very fresh / delicious
8 too salty / underdone

Exercise 7a

1 *c)*	3 d)	5 e)
2 f)	4 a)	6 b)

Exercise 7c

Possible answers

starter	tomato soup
main course	roast chicken with steamed vegetables
dessert	fruit salad and ice cream

4 Places in town

Exercise 1

1	b)	5	h)	9	g)
2	f)	6	a)	10	e)
3	l)	7	c)	11	d)
4	i)	8	j)	12	k)

Exercise 2a

police station	1	police station
shopping centre	2	shopping centre
post office	3	doctor's surgery
tourist information	4	bus station
department store	5	sports centre
art gallery	6	department store
bus station	7	job centre
job centre	8	post office
sports centre	9	art gallery
concert hall	10	railway station
doctor's surgery	11	tourist information
railway station	12	concert hall

Exercise 3a

C	O	U	R	T	B	A	N	K	S
S	D		H	C	L	U	B	U	U
C	C	I	N	E	M	A	N	O	P
H	S	A				I	O	E	E
O		C	H	T		V	K	R
O		O	O	R		E	S	M
L			T	E		R	H	A
M	U	S	E	U	M		S	O	R
C	O	L	L	E	G	E	I	P	K
L	A	U	N	D	R	E	T	T	E
	L	I	B	R	A	R	Y		T

Exercise 3b

the law
court

education
university
college
school

shops
supermarket
bookshop

services
bank
laundrette
hotel
(library)

culture and entertainment
cinema
museum
library
theatre
disco
club

Exercise 4

1 I'd go to the dentist's.
2 I'd go to the chemist's.
3 I'd go to the optician's.
4 I'd go to the laundrette.
5 I'd go to the dry cleaner's.
6 I'd go to the estate agent's.
7 I'd go to the supermarket.
8 I'd go to the police station.
9 I'd go to the job centre.
10 I'd go to the jeweller's.
11 I'd go to the bank.
12 I'd go to the florist's / flower shop.

Exercise 6

Possible answers

I'd like two tickets for Charlie's Angels please.
For the 6.30 performance, please.
Is there a discount for students?
I'll take tickets for 6.30, please.

Exercise 7

Dialogue 1

S / C	Order	
S	3	All washing machines come with a two-year guarantee. If you need any *help*, just ask
C	4	I will. Thank **you**.
S	1	Good morning. **Can** I help you?
C	2	I'm **just** looking, thanks.

Type of shop **electrical goods store**

Dialogue 2

S / C	Order	
S	3	Yes, we have. It's just **here**.
C	8	Could I **have** a receipt, please?
S	1	Are you **being** served?
S	7	Yes, of course you can. Sign **here**, please.
C	4	**How** much is it?
S	5	It's £12.99. It's on **special** offer.
C	2	No, I'm not. I'm **looking** for the latest Harry Potter book? Have you got it?
S	9	Of course. I'll **put** it in the bag with the book.
C	6	Oh, that's good. It's £15 in the other shops. **I'll** take it. Can I pay by credit **card**?

Type of shop **bookshop**

Dialogue 3

S / C	Order	
C	2	**I'll** take a lettuce, please.
S	1	Good morning, Mrs Harris. What **would** you like today?
S	5	Oh, yes. They came in this morning.
S	3	Anything **else**?
S	7	There you **are**. A lettuce and some carrots. Two pounds, please.
C	4	Yes, some carrots, please. Are they fresh?
C	8	I've only got a £20 note. Have you got any **change**?
C	6	In that case, I'll have a kilo.

Type of shop **greengrocer's**

5 Travel and transport

Exercise 1

1	information	5	way out
2	ticket office	6	refreshments
3	no smoking	7	buses and trains
4	left-luggage lockers	8	toilets

Exercise 2

1	get out	6	get off
2	get off	7	get in
3	catch	8	got on
4	take	9	get in
5	take off	10	land

Exercise 3

Possible answer

Last summer I travelled from … *to* … by train.
I bought a standard class return ticket. I've got a student card so I got a discount. The train left on time. It was a direct train to … . There was a buffet car so I had a sandwich. We arrived about five minutes early.

Exercise 4

	air travel	rail travel	bus travel
places and facilities	baggage reclaim check-in desk departure lounge terminal	buffet car left-luggage lockers station driver terminus waiting room	terminus station waiting room
people	pilot immigration officer cabin attendant	ticket collector driver	conductor ticket collector driver
tickets and documents	return boarding pass passport	return travel card pass (passport)	return travel card pass (passport)

Exercise 6

D	E	²P	A	³R	T	U	R	E	⁴S
O		L		R					T
	⁵W	A	I	T	I	⁶N	G		O
⁷R		T		⁸P		E			P
⁸O	F	F		⁹T		T			
O		O		I		¹⁰V			
M		¹¹R	E	C	L	A	I	¹²M	
	¹³P	M		K		N		¹⁴I	N
		E				E		L	
¹⁵T	I	¹⁶M	E	T	A	¹⁷B	L	E	¹⁸S
O		I				O			E
U		S		¹⁹C		A			A
²⁰R	E	S	²¹T	A	U	R	A	²²N	T
			²³O	R		D		O	

Exercise 7

terminal
airline
first class, business (or) economy
ticket (and your) passport
check in (your baggage and give you your) boarding pass
hand luggage
control (and through the) security (check)
departure (lounge and check which) gate (your) flight (leaves from)

6 Cinema, television and radio

Exercise 1

1	*animated* film	d
2	comedy	m
3	cartoon	g
4	gangster film	i
5	disaster movie	b
6	real-life drama	a
7	road movie	l
8	science fiction (sci-fi)	f
9	western	k
10	musical	n
11	love story	e
12	horror film	j
13	epic	h
14	thriller	c

Exercise 2

		☺	☹
1	It's very funny.	✔	
2	It's quite moving.	✔	
3	It's nonsense.		✔
4	It's a classic.	✔	
5	It's beautifully filmed.	✔	
6	The story is ridiculous.		✔
7	The acting is awful.		✔
8	He isn't very convincing.		✔
9	She's superb in the title role.	✔	
10	The animation is marvellous.	✔	

Exercise 4

1 *Turn up the brightness.*
2 Turn up the volume.
3 Turn up the colour.
4 Rewind it.
5 Fast-forward it.
6 Press the pause button. / Pause it

Exercise 5

That Thing	music programme / documentary
Learning Zone	educational programme
Oprah Winfrey	chat show
Hollyoaks	soap opera
The Animal Zone	wildlife programme
Top of the Pops	music programme
The Colourists	arts programme
Who Wants to be a Millionaire?	quiz show
Match of the Day	sports programme
Panorama	documentary

Exercise 7

Cinema
1 a) an epic
2 b) a comedy
3 b) a low-budget film
4 c) a classic

Radio
5 a) 97.6–99.8 Mhz
   b) Radio 1
   c) FM

TV
6 a) satellite
   b) cable
7 cartoons

7 Money

Exercise 1

	Notes	Coins
1	–	*£1+20p*
2	£20+£20+£5	50p
3	–	50p+20p+10p+5p
4	–	20p+2p+1p
5	–	£2+£1+50p+20p+20p
6	£10+£5	50p+20p+20p+5p+2p +2p

Exercise 2

```
      1  C  A  R  D
      2  N  U  M  B  E  R
         3  J  O  B
            4  B  R  O  K  E
      5  S  A  V  I  N  G  S
      6  T  I  L  L
      7  W  A  G  E
               8  P  O  C  K  E  T
      9  C  A  S  H  I  E  R
     10  A  L  L  O  W  A  N  C  E
     11  C  O  I  N  S
            12  C  H  E  Q  U  E
```

Exercise 3

1 c) cheque book
2 g) exchange rate
3 h) foreign currency
4 f) cash machine
5 a) savings account
6 d) travellers' cheques
7 e) debit card
8 b) weekly wage

Exercise 4

1	a)	Italy	lira
	b)	Spain	peseta
	c)	Russia	rouble
	d)	France	franc
	e)	Japan	yen
	f)	Argentina	peso
	g)	Morocco	dirham

2 eight
3 a cash machine
4 travellers' cheques
5 current account   savings account
6 Possible answers
   credit card   debit card   store card
7

```
BANK OF WORLD COMMERCE          Date 4th May
Pay The Clothes Company
Twenty-five pounds only            £ 25-00

0082746  65 74 90    1234 5678 00
```

8 commission
9 Possible answer
   How many lira are there to the English pound?
10 a receipt
11 exchange (or a) refund
12 salary

Exercise 5

1 a) babysitting
   b) delivering newspapers
   c) helping at the local hairdresser's
   d) helping on a market stall
   e) washing cars
   f) taking dogs for walks

5 a) cheque
   b) credit card / debit card
   c) store card
   d) savings account

8 Personal belongings, clothes and shoes

Exercise 1a

1 sunglasses
2 rollerblades
3 hairbrush
4 keyring
5 penknife
6 necklace
7 skateboard
8 earring

Exercise 2a

1 mobile phone
2 brief case
3 cheque book
4 glasses case
5 contact lenses
6 hair slide
7 address book
8 pencil case

Exercise 3

1 diary
2 ring
3 comb
4 calculator
5 CD player
6 bracelet
7 personal stereo
8 wallet
9 watch
10 rucksack

Exercise 4a

```
B O O T S   S     P
H E E L P I S A B L
S O L E O L L N U A
  C H E C K E D T T
W O O L K T E A T F
C L   Z E O V L O O
O L   I T E E S N R
T A S P O T T E D M
T R A I N E R S   S
O L E A T H E R
N     S T R I P E D
```

1 collar
2 sleeve
3 pocket
4 zip
5 button

Exercise 4b

Types of shoe		Materials	
6	boots	10	wool
7	trainers	11	cotton
8	sandals	12	silk
9	platforms	13	leather

Patterns		Parts of a shoe	
14	striped	17	heel
15	checked	18	sole
16	spotted	19	toe

Exercise 6
Possible answers

1 *It's a black leather jacket with two front pockets and a zip.*
2 It's a woollen jumper with plain sleeves and a patterned front.
3 It's a rucksack with a pocket on the front.
4 It's a checked shirt with a plain collar and two pockets.
5 It's a silver necklace with the letter E on it.

9 Phone, e-mail and letters

Exercise 1a

receiver
card
coins
dial

Exercise 1b
3 (Dial the area code, without the first '0'.)
1 (Dial the international code. From most countries, this is 00.)
4 (Dial the friend's number.)
2 (Dial the national code, which is 44.)

Exercise 1c
1 *police*   3 ambulance   5 operator
2 fire   4 directory enquiries

Exercise 2
1 *Speaking.*
2 Hold on
3 Can I take a message?
4 Do you want to hold?
5 I've got the wrong number.

Exercise 3
1 *post office*   6 e-mail address
2 answering machine   7 first class
3 directory enquiries   8 area code
4 air mail   9 wrong number
5 service provider   10 phone box / number

Exercise 4
1 *to*   *phone / e-mail*
2 up   phone
3 on   phone
4 up   phone / e-mail
5 up   phone
6 from   post
7 in   e-mail
8 in   e-mail
9 on   phone
10 back   phone

Exercise 5

	T		S	P	E	A	K	S	
P	O	S	T			G		P	U	T
R		E			T	A	K	E		O
I	N	T	O			I	N		N
N			P	H	O	N	E	D		E
T	E	X	T		R		N	W	
		I		D		G	R	
	C		O	P	E	R	A	T	O	R
S	O	O	N		R		G	N	
	D		S			E		G	O
K	E	Y		S	E	N	D	S		N

Exercise 6
C 9   Are you OK?
   10 (Do you) fancy going clubbing tonight?
   11 I could meet you at 7. See you later.
D 12 ... knows you are waiting.
   13 ... will be answered as soon as possible.
   14 ... try to connect you.

10 Holidays

Exercise 1
1 electricity hook-up   6 laundrette
2 cycle hire   7 wheelchair access
3 pony trekking   8 showers
4 phone   9 shop
5 *children's play area*

Exercise 2
Possible answers
Cornwall, in the south-west of England
on the coast
17 04 (year)
24 04 (year)
7
3
1 double room, 1 twin-bedded room,
1 single room
Is there wheelchair access?

Exercise 3
Travel   **Money**
1 *a package holiday*   6 a deposit
2 sightseeing   7 a tip
3 a tour   8 the bill
4 a guidebook   9 travellers' cheques
5 a phrase book

Places to stay
10 full board
11 a youth hostel
12 a cottage
13 a chalet
14 a bed and breakfast (B & B)
15 a caravan site / a campsite

Exercise 4b
Possible answers
Do you have any rooms available from ... to ...?
We'd like one twin-bedded and one single room, please.
Do all rooms have bathrooms en-suite?
Do we have to pay a deposit?

Exercise 5
1 *I'd like to check out please.*
2 I think there's something wrong with the shower.
3 Could I have a wake-up call, please?
4 What time is breakfast, please?

Exercise 6a
1 *spending*   7 trip
2 resort   8 sightseeing
3 touristy   9 took
4 hired   10 boring
5 sunbathing   11 sunny
6 picnic   12 pack

11 Landscape and weather

Exercise 1

	V	O	L	C	A	N	O			C	A	V	E
		A		L				M		O			B
		S		I				O		A			E
R	A	I	N	F	O	R	E	S	T		S			A
	E			S			F	I		T				C
	S						I	V		F	I	E	L	D
D	E	S	E	R	T			R		E				
	R					T		R		N			I	
	V	A	L	L	E	Y					I			
	O						E			S	T	R	E	A	M
H	I	L	L				A				L			
	R			A		O	C	E	A	N				
				K				D					
W	A	T	E	R	F	A	L	L					

Exercise 2a

stream   lake   waterfall
oasis   ocean   reservoir
river

Exercise 3a

1 Egypt	3 Tenerife	5 Japan
2 Switzerland	4 Venezuela	6 Poland

Exercise 4

1 *It's cold.*	4 It's freezing.	7 It's snowing.
2 It's hot.	5 It's foggy.	8 It's quite warm.
3 It's raining.	6 It's cloudy.	

Exercise 5

1 *thick*	4 scattered	6 heavy
2 a light	5 strong	7 lightning
3 sunny		

Exercise 6

Possible answers

Stockholm: In Stockholm today, there will be sunny periods. The top temperature will be 18°C. Tomorrow, there will be sunny periods with scattered showers. The temperature will rise to 19°C.

Moscow: In Moscow today, there will be strong winds. The top temperature will be 10°C. Tomorrow, there will be thick fog and the temperature will fall to 8°C.

Athens: In Athens today, there will be a good deal of sunshine. The top temperature will be 33°C. Tomorrow, there will be more sunshine, but there will also be a risk of thunder and lightning. The temperature will rise to 34°C.

Cairo: In Cairo today, there will be a good deal of sunshine with top temperatures of 34°C. Tomorrow, the sunshine will continue, and the temperature will rise to 40°C.

Barcelona: In Barcelona today, there will be sunny periods but it will be overcast for much of the day. The top temperature will be 28°C. Tomorrow, there will be quite heavy rain and the temperature will fall to 27°C.

12 The animal world

Exercise 1a

Exercise 1b

1	*dolphin*	11	shark
2	penguin	12	pig
3	alligator	13	lion
4	toad	14	sheep
5	frog	15	horse
6	donkey	16	duck
7	goose	17	ant
8	whale	18	fly
9	monkey	19	bee
10	hedgehog	20	rat

Exercise 2a

Possible answers for other animals in green

mammals	**fish**	**amphibians**
whale	shark	frog
monkey	salmon	toad
hedgehog	goldfish	newt
pig		salamander
lion	**reptiles**	
rat	alligator	**insects**
sheep	snake	ant
donkey	lizard	bee
horse		fly
dolphin	**birds**	mosquito
dog	goose	butterfly
cat	duck	
	penguin	
	eagle	
	swan	

Exercise 3

Possible answers

1 The spider is the odd one out because it is an invertebrate/has got eight legs/doesn't make noise/hasn't got fur.
2 The whale is the odd one out because it lives in the sea.
3 The frog is the odd one out because it's an amphibian.
4 The panda is the odd one out because it isn't a bird.
5 The wolf is the odd one out because it isn't a kind of cat.
6 The cow is the odd one out because it's an adult.
7 The worm is the odd one out because it can't fly.

Exercise 4

1	*chick*	*chicken, eggs*
2	calf	milk, beef
3	lamb	lamb
4	duckling	duck, eggs
5	gosling	goose, eggs
6	piglet	pork

Exercise 5

1 a) *goats*	6	c) a seal
2 c) a vampire bat	7	b) a spider
3 b) sharks	8	a) snails
4 a) a polar bear	9	c) a cheetah
5 b) a kangaroo	10	c) snakes

Test yourself 1 (Units 1 to 4)

Exercise 1

0	*forehead*	6	hair
1	eye	7	ear
2	nose	8	cheek
3	tooth / teeth	9	mouth
4	lip	10	neck
5	chin		

Exercise 2

0	*fair-skinned*
1	medium
2	bunches
3	oval
4	freckles

Exercise 3

Exercise 4

0	*cartons*	4	bottle
1	jar	5	packet
2	loaf	6	bar
3	tins		

Exercise 5

Things you find in a house

0 *work surface*
1 bath towel
2 linen basket
3 sound system
4 washing machine

Places in town

5 doctor's surgery
6 sports centre
7 art gallery
8 bowling alley
9 skating rink

Test yourself 2 (Units 5 to 8)

Exercise 1

0	*departures*	6	delayed
1	driver	7	arrivals
2	trip	8	timetable
3	board	9	train
4	miss	10	single
5	journey		

Exercise 2

0	*flight*	6	sunglasses
1	bus	7	trainers
2	travel card	8	rucksack
3	foreign currency	9	credit card
4	cash machine / ATM	10	watch
5	airport		

Exercise 3

Possible answers

1 *coach*, train, lorry, car, motorbike, scooter
2 *thriller*, western, horror film, disaster movie, cartoon, epic
3 *documentary*, sitcom, news, game show, chat show, sports programme
4 *taking dogs for walks*, washing cars, babysitting, helping on a market stall
5 *temporary job*, part-time job, summer job

Exercise 4

Possible answers

0 *nylon – I've got a nylon rucksack.*
1 plain – My plain jumper is my favourite.
2 beads – I don't like wearing things round my neck, so I never wear beads.
3 pocket – Put the keys in your pocket.
4 receipt – The shop assistant put the receipt in the bag.
5 coin – Have you got a £1 coin?
6 sitcom – Have you seen that new TV sitcom?
7 platform – Which platform does the train go from?
8 on time – It's OK, the train's on time.
9 conductor – The conductor will tell you when to get off the bus.
10 take off – What time does your plane take off?

Test yourself 3 (Units 9 to 12)

Exercise 1

0	e)	3	b)	6	i)
1	g)	4	a)	7	c)
2	d)	5	h)	8	f)

0 *I checked my e-mail but there were no messages for me.*
9 I booked a room at a hotel next to the beach.
10 I didn't return her call because I didn't have the number.
11 I went away for a long weekend.
12 I spent hours on the phone last night so that's why it was engaged for so long.
13 I paid the bill and left the hotel immediately.
14 I sent the parcel first class so you should get it tomorrow.
15 I called her number but there was no answer.
16 I can't stand package holidays because you have to do the same as everyone else.

Exercise 2

0	*hill*	0	*It's hot.*
1	mountain	6	It's snowing.
2	river	7	It's cloudy.
3	valley	8	It's raining.
4	lake	9	It's windy.
5	forest	10	It's sunny.

Exercise 3

0	*safari*	11	bats
1	lions	12	spider
2	tigers	13	north
3	giraffes	14	south
4	birds	15	beaches
5	butterflies	16	island
6	waterfall	17	lightning
7	elephant	18	tent
8	moon	19	lift
9	stars	20	camera
10	mosquitoes		

Exercise 4

Communications

0 *service* 1 class 2 mail 3 enquiries
4 tone 5 of

Weather

1 thunder 2 deal 3 showers 4 hard

Holidays

1 youth 2 trekking 3 site 4 B 5 service

Money you get or earn

pocket money .... (weekly) wage ....

allowance .... (annual) salary ....

I get £10 a week pocket money. ....

My parents give me spending money. ....

I get an allowance of £30 a month. ....

I get money for my birthday. ....

I get money for | doing chores around the house. ....

babysitting. ....

delivering newspapers. ....

taking dogs for walks. ....

helping on a market stall. ....

helping at the local hairdressers. ....

washing cars at the local supermarket. ....

(I've got)

a part-time job. .... I earn £20 a week.

a temporary job. ....

a summer job. .... I work part time.

a full-time job. ....

Expressions to do with money

I paid £50 for my watch. ....

I've spent too much money. ....

Can you lend me £10? ....

Could I borrow £10? ....

I owe you £10. ....

I save about £10 a month. ....

I put £10 a month into a savings account. ....

I'm broke. ....

My dad says I should save my spending money.

My mum says the same thing.

Why is it called 'spending money' if you have to save it?

Exactly.

REF *See page 87 for the British / American word list.*

1 Write down the fewest number of notes and coins you need to pay for these things without getting any change.

1 MAGAZINE £1.20

2 £45.50

3 £0.85

4 GUM £0.23

5 TRAVEL CARD SEC DGN SEAT 263 E 23 RETURN LONDON £3.90

6 £15.99

	Notes	Coins
1	—	£1 + 20p ....
2	....	....
3	....	....
4	....	....
5	....	....
6	....	....

2 Tracy's sister saves her pocket money. Solve the clues, and you will see what she is saving for.

1 Here's my credit .... (4)
2 My account .... is 2055883. (6)
3 I've got a part-time .... (3)
4 I haven't got any money. I'm completely .... (5)
5 Save some money. Open a .... account. (7)
6 Another word for the check-out in a store. (4)
7 Money paid for a week's work. (4)
8 I spend most of my .... money on computer games. (6)
9 He / She works in a bank. (7)
10 I get an .... of £40 a month. (9)
11 Money = notes and .... (5)
12 They don't accept credit cards, so I'll write a .... (6)

1 | C | A | R | D
2
3
4
5
6
7
8
9
10
11
12

3 Match the words in column A with those in column B.

A			B
1 cheque	..c)..	cheque book	a) account
2 exchange	....	....	b) wage
3 foreign	....	....	c) book
4 cash	....	....	d) cheques
5 savings	....	....	e) card
6 travellers'	....	....	f) machine
7 debit	....	....	g) rate
8 weekly	....	....	h) currency

4   Answer the questions in the Money Quiz.

MONEY QUIZ

How much do you know about money?

1 Match the countries with the currencies.

a)	Italy	rouble
b)	Spain	lira
c)	Russia	franc
d)	France	peso
e)	Japan	dirham
f)	Argentina	yen
g)	Morocco	peseta

2 How many different coins are there in English money?

....

3 What is another name for an ATM?

....

4 What do you call cheques which you can change at banks in other countries?

....

5 Name two types of account you can have at a bank.

....

6 Name two types of card which you can use to pay in a shop.

....

7 It's 4th May. You want to write a cheque for £25 to The Clothes Company. Fill in the cheque.

8 What do you call the amount the bank charges to change money from one currency to another?

....

9 In a bank, how do you ask about the exchange rate between your currency and the English pound?
How many ....
....?

10 In a shop, what do you ask for to prove that you have bought something?

....

11 You buy a T-shirt but it is too small so you take it back to the shop. The shop assistant should offer you an

.... or a ....

12 A wage is the amount you earn in a week. What do you call the amount you earn in a year?

....

Answers

Check your answers on page E. Then read the analysis below.

ANALYSIS

12 correct	Do you work in a bank?
8-11 correct	You know about money. Are you good at Maths, too?
5-10 correct	Not bad.
0-4 correct	You aren't interested in money, are you? You're an artist, a musician or a writer, perhaps.

5 Fill in the questionnaire.

GETTING AND SPENDING MONEY

1 Write the words for the jobs. Tick the ones which you would do.

☐ a *babysitting*...................
☐ b ....
☐ c ....
☐ d ....
☐ e ....
☐ f ....

2 How and when do you get money?
....
....

3 Do you save money?
....
How much do you save per month?
....
Where do you put it?
....

4 Which of these things have you bought in the last week? What was the equivalent cost in English money?

☐ ....
☐ ....
☐ ....
☐ ....
☐ ....
☐ ....
☐ ....
☐ ....
☐ ....
☐ ....
☐ ....
☐ ....
☐ ....
☐ ....

TOTAL COST: ....

5 Write the words and tick the ones you have.

a .... ☐

c .... ☐

b .... ☐

d .... ☐

6 Tick the statements you agree with and put a cross after those you disagree with. Add any comments you wish.

a You should never lend anyone money. ☐

....

b You should never borrow money. ☐

....

c You should never owe money. ☐

....

d If you borrow money, you should pay it back as soon as you can. ☐

....

e You should never spend more than you've got. ☐

....

f If a friend needs money, you should always lend or give it to them. ☐

....

g If you see something you like, you should always buy it. ☐

....

7 How would you describe yourself?

a) generous ☐ b) mean ☐ c) careful with money ☐ d) careless with money ☐

6 Write ten words and five expressions you are going to memorize.

Words	Expressions
1	1 ....
2	....
3	2 ....
4	....
5	3 ....
6	....
7	4 ....
8	....
9	5 ....
10	....

8 Personal belongings, clothes and shoes

Translate the words and phrases.

Everyday items

bag	....
rucksack	....
school bag	....
brief case	....
mobile phone	....
umbrella	....
wallet	....
purse	....
cheque book	....
credit card	....
keys	....
keyring	....
glasses	....
glasses case	....
sunglasses	....
contact lenses	....
calculator	....
diary	....

personal organiser / 'Filofax' ™	....
address book	....
watch	....
CD (compact disc)	....
CD player	....
minidisc	....
minidisc player	....
personal stereo / 'walkman' ™	....
rollerskates	....
rollerblades	....
skateboard	....
pen	....
pencil case	....
penknife	....
hairbrush	....
comb	....

Types of shoe

trainers	....
boots	....
high heels	....
platforms	....
flat shoes	....
lace-ups	....
slip-ons	....
sandals	....
plimsolls	....
espadrilles	....

Jewellery and accessories

earring	....
stud	....
bracelet	....
(silver) ring	....
brooch	....
(gold) chain	....
necklace	....
beads	....
hair slide	....

Parts of a shoe

laces ....   heel ....

toe ....   sole ....

REF See *Boost your Vocabulary 1*, Clothes, page 65, for parts of clothes.

Materials

cotton ....
denim ....
silk ....
wool ....
nylon ....
canvas ....
leather ....
suede ....
plastic ....
manmade ....
synthetic ....

> *The materials (**cotton** ... **plastic**) are used as both nouns and adjectives. **Manmade** and **synthetic** are only adjectives. **Wool** has two adjectives: **wool** and **woollen**.*

Patterns

plain ....

patterned ....

striped ....

checked ....

spotted ....

My most important belongings are my mobile phone and my diary. ....
....
I take my skateboard almost everywhere! ....
I usually wear a gold chain, but I don't wear any other jewellery. ....
....
My favourite jacket is my baseball jacket. ....
It's white with red sleeves. It's got the number 49 on the back. ....
....
Where did you get your leather jacket with all the zips? It's cool. ....
....
I like that striped woollen jumper. ....
I've got a patterned canvas rucksack with pockets. ....

It's a spotted cotton shirt with big buttons, short sleeves and a plain collar. It's so uncool.

> REF
> See page 87 for the British / American word list.

1a Join a word from column A to a word from column B to make a new word.

1b Tick (✔) the items you have.

A	B
1 sun	a) brush
2 roller	b) ring
3 hair	c) lace
4 key	d) glasses
5 pen	e) board
6 neck	f) ring
7 skate	g) knife
8 ear	h) blades

1 *sunglasses* .... ☐
2 .... ☐
3 .... ☐
4 .... ☐
5 .... ☐
6 .... ☐
7 .... ☐
8 .... ☐

2a Match a word from column A with a word from column B. (Write them as separate words.)

2b Tick (✔) the items you have.

A	B
1 mobile	a) book
2 brief	b) lenses
3 cheque	c) case
4 glasses	d) slide
5 contact	e) book
6 hair	f) case
7 address	g) case
8 pencil	h) phone

1 *mobile phone* .... ☐
2 .... ☐
3 .... ☐
4 .... ☐
5 .... ☐
6 .... ☐
7 .... ☐
8 .... ☐

3a Complete the words.

3b Tick (✔) the items you have.

1 d *i a r y* ☐   4 c _ _ _ _ _ _ _ _ ☐   7 p _ _ _ _ _ _ _ s _ _ _ _ _ ☐

2 r _ _ _ ☐   5 CD p _ _ _ _ _ ☐   8 w _ _ _ _ _ ☐

3 c _ _ _ ☐   6 b _ _ _ _ _ _ ☐   9 w _ _ _ _ ☐   10 r _ _ _ _ _ _ _ ☐

If you are working in class, give your partner one minute to look at your answers to exercises 1, 2 and 3. Then ask:

What have I got?

4a Match the five circled words in the wordsearch to the pictures below.

T	B	O	O	T	S	E	S	N	P
H	E	E	L	P	I	S	A	B	L
S	O	L	E	O	L	L	N	U	A
I	C	H	E	C	K	E	D	T	T
W	O	O	L	K	T	E	A	T	F
C	L	P	Z	E	O	V	L	O	O
O	L	M	I	T	E	E	S	N	R
T	A	S	P	O	T	T	E	D	M
T	R	A	I	N	E	R	S	H	S
O	L	E	A	T	H	E	R	D	W
N	L	C	S	T	R	I	P	E	D

1  *collar*..............................

2  ....

3  ....

4  ....

5  ....

4b Now find and match...

- four words for types of shoe
- four words for materials
- three words for patterns
- three words for parts of a shoe

Types of shoe

6  ....

7  ....

8  ....

9  ....

Materials

10  ....

11  ....

12  ....

13  ....

Patterns

14  ....

15  ....

16  ....

Parts of a shoe

17  ....

18  ....

19  ....

5a Write a list of the ten items that are most important to you.

5b What do you think your best friend's top ten items are? Write a list.

6 Imagine you have lost these items. You are describing them to the lost-property officer. Write the descriptions.

1 *It's a black leather jacket with two front pockets and a zip.*

2 ....

3 ....

4 ....

5 ....

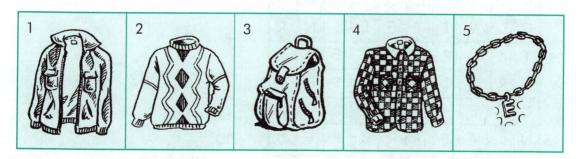

7 These are the top ten lost items in the UK. But what order should they be in? Write down your guesses.

(1 = the thing that is most often lost)

The top ten lost items

1	6 ....
2	7 ....
3	8 ....
4	9 ....
5	10 ....

8a Read the list of the top ten lost items.
How many did you guess correctly?   Answer: ....

The top ten lost items

1 clothes
19,000

2 mobile phones
13,000

3 umbrellas
11,000

4 purses
11,000

5 credit cards
10,500

6 school bags
9,000

7 other bags
8,900

8 keys
8,900

9 glasses
7,000

10 cheque books
4,800

Source: Daily Telegraph T2

8b Tick the items you have lost in the past year.
Is there anything else you've lost?

I've also lost ....

9 Write ten words and five expressions you are going to memorize.

Words	Expressions
1	1 ....
2	....
3	2 ....
4	....
5	3 ....
6	....
7	4 ....
8	....
9	5 ....
10	....

Test yourself 2 (Units 5 to 8)

How much can you remember?

1 Find ten words to do with travel.

D	E	P	A	R	T	U	R	E	S
E	P	O	R	I	I	L	T	K	I
L	J	H	R	X	M	A	R	Q	N
A	D	R	I	V	E	R	A	S	G
Y	M	N	V	B	T	R	I	P	L
E	C	L	A	U	A	B	N	T	E
D	E	I	L	E	B	O	A	R	D
M	I	S	S	O	L	J	V	L	R
J	O	U	R	N	E	Y	U	S	Z

0 ....departures..
1 ....
2 ....
3 ....
4 ....
5 ....
6 ....
7 ....
8 ....
9 ....
10 ....

(10 marks)

2 Use the pictures to complete the entry in Sophie's diary.

I was so excited about my holiday in Greece! My ⁰ ....*flight*....... wasn't until 4.30 in the afternoon, so I went into town to get some things I needed for the holiday. I caught the ¹ .... at about ten o'clock. I bought a ² .... because I wanted to use the underground as well. I needed some English money and some ³ .... for when I first arrived in Crete, but when I got to the bank it was closed. Then I remembered. It was Saturday. Luckily there's a ⁴ .... in the wall outside the bank, so I could at least get some English money. And I knew I could change money at the ⁵ .... I went straight into the Metro shopping centre. The sun is quite strong in Greece so I wanted to get some good ⁶ .... I tried lots on before I found some I liked. Then I saw a pair of really cool ⁷ .... in a sports shop. I just had to have them. I came out of the sports shop and saw a canvas and leather ⁸ .... in the window of a shop which just sells bags.

It was quite expensive. I didn't have enough money to buy it, so I used my ⁹ .... It was then that I looked at my ¹⁰ .... It was 4.30. I'd missed my plane.

(10 marks)

3 Write ...

  1 **five more types of vehicle**
    coach ....

  2 **five more types of film**
    thriller ....

  3 **five more types of TV programme**
    documentary ....

  4 **three more ways of earning pocket money**
    taking dogs for walks ....

  5 **two more types of job**
    temporary job ....

(20 marks)

4 Underline the odd one out. Then use it in a phrase or a sentence.

  0 silk   wool   leather   <u>nylon</u>
     I've got a nylon rucksack. ....

  1 denim   plain   cotton   wool
    ....

  2 beads   slip-ons   plimsolls   lace-ups
    ....

  3 pocket   toe   heel   sole
    ....

  4 salary   wage   allowance   receipt
    ....

  5 credit   store   coin   debit
    ....

  6 western   epic   thriller   sitcom
    ....

  7 boarding pass gate   platform   baggage reclaim
    ....

  8 cancelled   on time   delayed   late
    ....

  9 conductor   pilot   flight attendant   immigration officer
    ....

  10 get on   get off   take off   change
    ....

(20 marks)

9 Phone, e-mail and letters

Translate the words and phrases.

Telephones

phone box	....
phone card	....
mobile phone	....
(star) key	....
cordless phone	....
handset / receiver	....
answering machine	....

Numbers and services

international code	....
national code	....
area code	....
operator	....
directory enquiries	....
fire	
police	....
ambulance	....

Phoning

to ring / phone / call someone	....
to call / dial (a number)	....
to call back	....
to return a call	....
to hang up	....
to put the phone down (on someone)	....
to send a text message	....
to pick up your messages	....
to monitor your calls	....
to key in (your account number)	....
Can you speak up, please?	....
What's your phone number?	....
Sorry, you've got the wrong number.	....
I spend hours on the phone.	....

It's	ringing.	....	It's	out of order.	....
	engaged.	....		a bad line.	....

Talking on the phone

A: Hello. Is (Will) there, please? ....

B: Yes, (he) is. Hold on, I'll (just) get ....
(him) for you. ....

A: Can I speak to (Jane), please? ....

B: Sorry, (she) isn't here. ....
Can I take a message? / ....

B: Sorry, (she's) on the other line. ....
Do you want to hold? ....

A: Is that (Tim)? ....

B: Speaking.

Sending letters

post office	....
letter	....
PS (postscript)	....
envelope	....
package	....
parcel	....
postcard	....
address	....
postcode	....
first class stamp	....
second class stamp	....
post box	....
air mail	....
delivery	....
collection	....
postman / postwoman	....

I sent it first class. ....

Has the post arrived yet? ....

I got / had a letter from Claire this morning. ....

I haven't heard from my uncle for ages. ....

What time does the post go? ....

Sending e-mails (verbs)

type in your password	....
check your e-mail(s)	....
send an e-mail / a message	....
get an e-mail	....
forward an e-mail	....
print out an e-mail	....
be online	....
surf the net	....
We keep in touch by e-mail.	....
Who's your internet service provider (ISP)?	....
What's your e-mail address?	....
I can't open this attachment.	....

tracy@teenmail.com
'My e-mail address is: Tracy at teenmail dot com; all lower case.'

Automated phone services

The person you are calling knows you are waiting.

If you have a touch-tone telephone, please press the star key now.

You will now hear a series of options.

Your call is in a queue and will be answered as soon as possible.

Please hold while we try to connect you.

Please try again later.

If you leave a message we'll get back to you as soon as possible.

Please speak clearly after the long tone.

REF

See page 84 for information about the postal service in Britain.

REF

See page 87 for the British / American word list.

9

1a Complete the instructions.

> **How to make a phone call from a phone box in Britain**
>
> Lift the r e c e i v e r.
>
> Put in your phone c_ _ _ or some c_ _ _ _.
>
> D_ _ _ the number.

1b Put the instructions in the correct order.

> **How to make a call from another country to a friend in Britain**
>
> ..... Dial the area code, without the first '0'.
>
> ..1.. Dial the international code. From most countries, this is 00.
>
> ..... Dial the friend's number.
>
> ..... Dial the national code, which is 44.

1c Write in the telephone services.

> BANK
>
> 1 *police* ....
>
> 2 ....
>
> 3 ....
>
> 4 ....
>
> ....
>
> 5 ....

2 Write the missing phrases and sentences in these conversations.

1 – Is Mr Young there, please?
– *Speaking*..............
– Oh, hello, Mr Young.

2 – Hello. Is Karim there, please?
– Yes, he is. ....,
I'll just get him for you.

3 – Hello. Can I speak to Juliet, please?
– Sorry, she isn't here. ....
....?
– Yes, if you could. Just say that Tom called and ask her to ring me.

4 – Is Mrs Palmer there, please?
– I'm afraid she's on the other line.
....?
– No, it's OK. I'll call back later.

5 – Is that 7584 9376?
– No, this is 7584 9377.
– Oh, sorry, ...
....

3 Match the words in A with the words in B.

A		B	
1 post	6 e-mail	address	machine
2 answering	7 first	code	mail
3 directory	8 area	class	number
4 air	9 wrong	box	office
5 service	10 phone	enquiries	provider

1 *post office* ....
2 ....
3 ....
4 ....
5 ....
6 ....
7 ....
8 ....
9 ....
10 ....

4 Choose a word in the box to complete the sentences. You will need to use some words more than once. Then write *post*, *phone* or *e-mail* to show the context of each sentence.

back	up	from	in	to	on

Post / phone / e-mail

1 I'll get back ……………*to*………… you as soon as possible. *phone / e-mail*
2 Please hang …………………… ……………………………………
3 She's ……………………… the other line. ……………………………………
4 I need to pick …………………… my messages. ……………………………………
5 Can you speak …………………… please? ……………………………………
6 I had a postcard …………………… Jonathon. ……………………………………
7 We keep …………………… touch by e-mail. ……………………………………
8 Type …………………… your password. ……………………………………
9 Hold ……………………, I'll get him for you. ……………………………………
10 I'll call …………………… later. ……………………………………

5 Solve the crossword.

Across ▶

2 She … to him on the phone every day. (5)
5 I'll send her an e-mail. It'll be quicker than the … .(4)
7 He was so rude. He … the phone down on me. (3)
9 I'm afraid she's not here. Can I … a message? (4)
10 I'll take the phone … the other room. (4)
12 Another word for *called* or *rang*. (6)
15 On my mobile phone, you can receive voice messages or … messages. (4)
18 If you think Karen's number is out of order, ask the … to check it. (8)
19 If you leave a message, we'll get back to you as … as possible. (4)
20 What time does the post … ? (2)
22 Please … in your account number. (3)
23 He always … her a birthday card. (5)

Down ▼

1 Do you want … hold, caller? (2)
2 Short for 'Street'. (2)
3 Please try … later. (5)
4 How long do you … on the phone each day? (5)
5 I … out e-mails if I want to keep them. (5)
6 'Hand…' is another word for receiver. (3)
8 Please speak clearly after the long … . (4)
11 You will now hear a series of … . (7)
13 When I dial the number, nothing happens. Her phone must be out of … .(5)
14 You're popular! Your phone's been … for hours! (7)
16 Sorry, I've got the … number. (5)
17 Before the local number, you must dial the area … . (4)
21 Sorry, he's … the other line. (2)

Crossword grid (Across 2): S P E A K S

9

6 Answer the questions.

Are you a good communicator?

A Have you used any of these things in the last week? How many times?

Yes. I've used a phone several times.
....
No. I haven't used a mobile phone.
....

1 ....
2 ....
3 ....

B a) Have you *sent* any of these things in the last week? How many? / Who to?
**   b) Have you *received* any of these things in the last week? How many / Who to?**

4 a) ....
   ....
   b) ....
   ....

5 a) ....
   ....
   b) ....
   ....

6 a) ....
   b) ....
   ....

7 a) ....
   ....
   b) ....
   ....

8 a) ....
   ....
   b) ....
   ....

C Can you understand these text messages? Write them out in full.

9 RUOK?

....

10 FanC goin clubN 2nite?

....

11 I c%d mEt U @ 7. CUL8R.

....

D What comes next in these automated service messages?

12 'The person you are calling ....
....'

13 'Your call is in a queue and ....
....'

14 'Please hold while we ....
....'

ANALYSIS

Sections A and B

9 – 13 'Yes' answers:

You're a very good communicator, and you like technology.

6 – 8 'Yes' answers:

You're quite a good communicator, and you're OK with technology.

1 – 5 'Yes' answers:

Either you're so popular that you don't need to get in touch with people (they get in touch with you); or you prefer communicating with people face-to-face.

Section C Answers

Are you OK?

(Do you) fancy going clubbing tonight?

I could meet you at seven. See you later.

Three correct answers:	See you at seven.
Two correct answers:	Number 3 was the problem, eh?
One correct answer:	OK, so you don't want to go clubbing …
No correct answers:	Did you know that you can get a text-messaging dictionary?

Section D

If you got all of these right: You need to get off the phone and get out more!

---

7 Write ten words and five expressions you are going to memorize.

Words	Expressions
1	1 ....
2	....
3	2 ....
4	....
5	3 ....
6	....
7	4 ....
8	....
9	5 ....
10	....

10 Holidays

Translate the words and phrases.

Time off

to take time off ....

to go away for a long weekend ....

to have a holiday ....

to go on holiday ....

to spend three weeks in (Spain) ....

Types of holiday

to go ...

   to a resort ....

   to the mountains ....

   to the countryside ....

   on a package
    holiday ....

   on a beach holiday ....

to go ...

   on a tour ....

   on safari ....

   skiing ....

   walking ....

   camping ....

   sightseeing ....

Preparing to go

ticket ....

passport ....

phrase book ....

guidebook ....

travellers' cheques ....

to pack your bag ....

camera ....

Accommodation

to stay at a ...

   hotel ....

   bed and breakfast
   ('B & B') ....

   youth hostel ....

   campsite ....

   caravan site ....

to rent a/an ...

   cottage ....

   villa ....

   apartment ....

   chalet ....

Staying at a campsite

tent ....

caravan ....

pitch (= space for
 a tent) ....

electricity hook-up ....

gas ....

restaurant ....

café ....

bar ....

showers ....

shop ....

laundrette ....

phone ....

children's play area ....

swimming pool ....

fishing ....

mini-golf /
 crazy golf ....

pony trekking ....

tennis courts ....

table tennis ....

cycle hire ....

wheelchair access ....

Staying in a hotel

to book ....
to pay a deposit ....
half board (includes breakfast and dinner)
....
full board (includes breakfast, lunch and dinner)
....
reception ....
receptionist ....
lift *(noun)* ....
room service ....
reservation ....
first floor ....
key ....
tip *(noun / verb)* ....

a room with a ...
  bathroom (en suite) ....
  shower ....
  TV ....
  telephone ....
  sea view ....

a single room ....
a double room
  (= with a double bed) ....
a twin-bedded room
  (= with two beds) ....

REF *See page 87 for the British / American word list.*

Do you have any rooms available? ....
We'd like to stay for two nights. ....
What time is breakfast, please? ....
Could I have a wake-up call, please? ....
Could I put it (e.g. a drink) on the bill, please? ....
I'd like to check in / out, please. ....
I'd like to pay the bill, please. ....
Excuse me. The television doesn't work. / ....
I think there's something wrong with the shower. ....

Describing a holiday

Activities

sunbathing ....
swimming ....
relaxing ....
sightseeing ....
We went on an excursion.
....
We went on a boat trip.
....
We took photos.
....
We had a picnic.
....
We hired bikes.
....

Impressions

beautiful ....
quiet ....
lively ....
crowded ....
touristy ....
boring ....
We had a great time.
....
It was sunny. / It rained the whole time.
....
The weather was fantastic / terrible.
....
The food was lovely / disgusting.
....

1 Complete the list of facilities.

BUENA VISTA CAMPSITE

1........................

2........................

3........................

4........................

5 *children's play area*

6........................

7........................

8........................

9........................

2 Fill in the online booking form.

We want to find a B & B on the coast in Cornwall, in the south-west of England. There are five of us: my husband, myself, our two children Jonathon (fifteen) and Jessica (eighteen), and my mother. The children don't mind sharing a room. My mother sometimes uses a wheelchair. She'd like a room overlooking the sea. We want to go for a week from Friday 17 April, returning Friday 24 April.

HOTELS AND B & Bs

Country / Area..

....

Location...

Check in: .... Day .... Month .... Year

Check out: .... Day .... Month .... Year

Number of nights..

Rooms..

Types of room..

....

Special needs / Questions..........................

....

One of our travel advisors will confirm your reservation request within one working day and will send you an e-mail giving details of the booking terms and amount due.

3 Try this quiz.

HOLIDAY QUIZ

Travel

What do you call ...

1   a holiday where travel and accommodation are included in the price?
    a package holiday

2   a holiday looking at places of interest?

....

3   a holiday which includes a number of destinations?

....

4   a book which tells you about places to visit?

....

5   a book which gives you useful words and phrases to use on holiday?

....

Money

What do you call ...

6   the money you pay before arriving at a hotel or campsite, to book your room or place?

....

7   the extra money you give to a waiter or a taxi driver?

....

8   the piece of paper which tells you how much you have to pay?

....

9   cheques which can be used in any country?

....

Places to stay

What do you call ...

10   accommodation with all meals?

....

11   a place which is not expensive and where mostly young people stay?

....

12   a small old house in the country?

....

13   a wooden house in or near a ski resort?

....

14   a house or small hotel where the only meal provided is breakfast?

....

15   a place where you can park a caravan?

....

Holidays and you

16   Which of these holidays would you choose, and why?

....
....
....

17   Where do you usually go on holiday?

....

18   What do you normally do on holiday?

....

Answers

Check your answers on page F.

4a You are going to England for a holiday with your friends. You find a youth hostel on the Internet and you phone to make a reservation. First complete the notes.

Number in your group:	Types of room:	Check-in date:	Questions:
....	....	....	....
Number of rooms:	....	**Check-out date:**	....
....	....	....	....

4b Now write your part of the telephone conversation.

Receptionist: Holland Park Youth Hostel, good morning.
You: *(Rooms available? Dates)* ....
....

Receptionist: Yes, we do. What exactly do you require?
You: *(Number and types of room)* ....
....

Receptionist: Yes, that's fine. We can do that.
You: *(Special needs / Questions)* ....
....

Receptionist: Yes.
You: *(Deposit?)* ....
....

Receptionist: Yes, please. If you can give me your credit card details ...

5 Write what the people are saying.

1 *I'd like to check out, please.*
....
....

3 Could ....
....
....
....
....

2 Hello, this is Room 202.
....
....
....

4 What ....
....
....
....
....

6a Wayne went with his family on holiday last year. Use the words in the box to complete his postcard.

resort	hired	pack	picnic	spending	took
sightseeing	touristy	trip	sunny	boring	sunbathing

Dear Tracy

We're 1 ....spending...... a week at a 2 .... on the coast.
There are lots of plastic donkeys and silly hats in the shops, because it's
a really 3 .... place. I think it's horrible, but you'd like it.
        I 4 .... a bike on Monday, but I fell off
and hurt my leg. I wanted to try waterskiing or windsurfing,
but I can't now.
        Yesterday, Mum and Dad just lay on the beach 5 ....
all morning. Then we had a 6 .... , but it was too hot and
there were lots of flies. I wanted to go on a boat 7 .... in the
afternoon, but we went 8 .... instead. They 9 ....
lots of photos, but I thought it was really 10 .... Even the
weather's boring: it's just 11 .... the whole time.
        I can't wait to 12 .... my bag and go home.

Wayne

ADDRE

6b Write a postcard from somewhere you've been on holiday.

7 Write ten words and five expressions you are going to memorize.

Words	Expressions
1	1 ....
2	....
3	2 ....
4	....
5	3 ....
6	....
7	4 ....
8	....
9	5 ....
10	....

Landscape and weather

Translate the words and phrases.

The earth

continent	....
country	....
island	....
peninsula	....
ocean	....
sea	....
land	....

The sky

sun	....
moon	....
star	....
planet	....
space	....

Points of the compass

north ....

north west ....   north east ....

west ....   east ....

south west ....   south east ....

south ....

I live in the north of England. ....

My village is ten kilometres east of York. ....

Landscape features

bay	....	stream	....
beach	....	canal	....
cave	....	tree	....
cliff	....	valley	....
rock	....	wood	....
coast	....	mountain	....
coastline	....	mountain range	....
field	....	desert	....
forest	....	oasis	....
hill	....	plain	....
lake	....	rainforest	....
pond	....	volcano	....
reservoir	....	waterfall	....
river	....		

REF *See page 84 in the reference section for the use of the definite article with named landscape features.*

Weather

It's | cold. | ....
| chilly. | ....
| frosty. | ....
| freezing. | ....
| snowing. | ....
| hailing. | ....
| hot. | ....
| warm. | ....
| sunny. | ....
| humid. | ....
| misty. | ....
| foggy. | ....
| cloudy. | ....
| stormy. | ....
| windy. | ....
| raining. | ....

It's pouring! ....
I'm boiling! ....
I'm freezing! ....

What's the weather like?
....

Is it going to rain / snow?
....

I think there's going to be a storm.
....

Aren't you cold?

Me, cold? Of course not. I'm tough.

See page 84 for Celsius and Fahrenheit.

Weather forecasts

There will be ...
   a good deal of sunshine.
....
   sunny periods.
....
   strong winds.
....
   a light breeze.
....
   heavy rain.
....
   scattered showers.
....
   drizzle.
....
   thunder and lightning.
....
   thick fog.
....
   a hard frost.
....

It will be ...
   overcast. ....
   a dull day. ....
   mild. ....
   wet. ....

Temperatures will rise to 27°C
(degrees centigrade).
....

Temperatures will fall to minus 2°C.
....

The early-morning mist will gradually clear.
....

There's a risk of thunder later on in the day.
....

See page 87 for the British / American word list.

1 Complete the grid with landscape words.

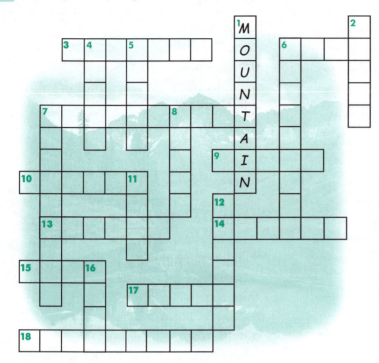

Down ▼

1 A very high hill, which often has snow on the top. (8)

2 A sandy area next to the sea. (5)

4 An area of water in *10 Across*. (5)

5 A high rock which goes straight down to the sea. (5)

6 The line between the land and the sea. (9)

7 A large manmade area of water. (9)

8 A natural line of water that runs across a country to the sea. (5)

11 A tall plant which lives for many years. (4)

12 An area of land with water all around it. (6)

16 A large natural area of water with land all around it. (4)

Across ▶

3 A mountain with a large hole at the top, which can be dangerous if it's active. (7)

6 A large natural hole in rock. (4)

7 A large area of trees in a tropical climate. (10)

9 A grassy area where you often see cows or sheep. (5)

10 A large area of sand where it is always hot and dry. (6)

13 A low area between two lines of hills or mountains. (6)

14 A small river. (6)

15 An area of land that is higher than the land around it. (4)

17 The large area of salt water that covers most of the earth. (5)

18 Water that falls straight down over a high rock. (9)

2a Look again at the grid. List the words to do with water.

stream ....

....

2b Which of the landscape features in the grid are within one hundred kilometres of your home? Make a list, with their names, and add any that are not in the grid, e.g. canal, forest.

Feature *Name*
beach Teresitas Beach

3a Where is it? Choose from the places in the box.

| Japan | Egypt | Switzerland | Poland | Tenerife | Venezuela |

QUICK QUIZ *How good is your geography?*

1 Perhaps you want to travel down the River Nile, visit the pyramids or the Valley of the Kings, or maybe even go into the Sahara Desert. If you like water, you can choose between the Mediterranean Sea in the north and the Red Sea in the east.

....

2 If you like mountains, you can go to the Alps or the Jura mountains. You can go sailing on Lake Lucerne or Lake Geneva and you can walk in the beautiful valleys, but there's no sea for you to swim in because this country doesn't have a coastline.

....

3 It's an island close to the north-west coast of Africa, but it isn't part of Africa. It's got an active volcano in the centre called Pico de Teide. It's a popular holiday destination.

....

4 In this South American country, you'll find the world's highest waterfall, Angel Falls. You can go walking in the Andes, which are in the north-west of the country, or you can stay in the central plains and explore the Orinoco river. Or maybe you want to enjoy life in the capital, Caracas.

....

5 This country is in the Pacific Ocean. It's made up of over a thousand islands. The landscape is mostly made up of mountains. There's a volcano called Mount Fuji.

....

6 Most of the country is quite flat, but in the south there are the Carpathian mountains. You can go walking and skiing there. In the east there are large forests. In the north-east there are several lakes, but the only coastline is in the north. That's where you'll find the Baltic Sea.

....

ANSWERS
Check your answers on page G.

3b Write a similar description of your own country, or a country you know. Remember to use landscape words.

4 Use the sentences in the box to describe the weather in each picture.

| It's foggy. | It's freezing. | It's hot. | It's raining. |
| It's cold. | It's snowing. | It's quite warm. | It's cloudy. |

1 *It's cold.*

2 ....

3 ....

4 ....

5 ....

6 ....

7 ....

8 ....

5 Choose the correct word to complete the weather forecast.

1 thick / heavy
2 light / a light
3 sun / sunny
4 a light / scattered
5 heavy / strong
6 thick / heavy
7 light / lightning

In the north there will be [1] *thick* .... fog in the early part of the day, but this will clear towards midday. In the afternoon, there will be [2] .... breeze and some [3] .... periods, although there is a risk of [4] .... showers tomorrow evening. Overnight, there will be [5] .... winds with [6] .... rain and even a risk of thunder and [7] ....

6 Look at the weather forecast for today and tomorrow in Berlin. Then write the forecasts for Stockholm, Moscow, Athens, Cairo and Barcelona.

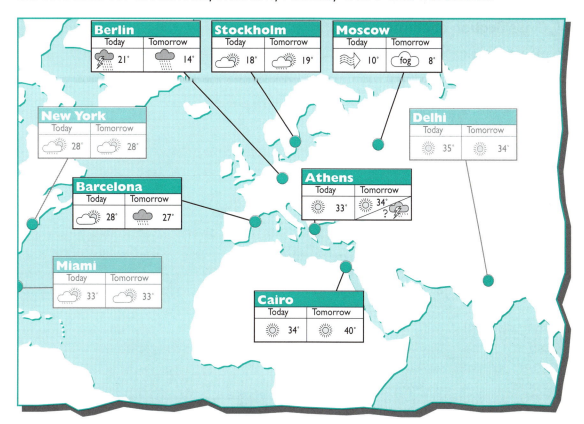

Berlin

In Berlin today, there will be thunder and lightning. There will also be heavy rain. The top temperature will be 21°C. Tomorrow, the rain will continue. It will be overcast and the temperature will fall to 14°C.

7 Write ten words and five expressions you are going to memorize.

Words		Expressions	
1	....	1	....
2	....		....
3	....	2	....
4	....		....
5	....	3	....
6	....		....
7	....	4	....
8	....		....
9	....	5	....
10	....		....

The animal world

Translate the words and phrases.

Classification of animals

mammals, e.g. horse, bear	....
birds, e.g. duck, eagle	....
reptiles, e.g. alligator, crocodile	....
amphibians, e.g. frog, toad	....
fish, e.g. goldfish, salmon	....
invertebrates e.g. insects, spiders	....

Farm animals

Adult

		Young	
cow	....	calf (calves)	....
horse	....	foal	....
duck	....	duckling	....
goose (geese)	....	gosling	....
hen	....	chick	....
sheep (sheep)	....	lamb	....
pig	....	piglet	....
goat	....	kid	....
donkey	....		

 REF See also **Boost Your Vocabulary 1**, *Pets, page 39.*

Other common animals

ant	....
bee	....
butterfly	....
cockroach	....
fly	....
mosquito	....
mouse (mice)	....
pigeon	....
rat	....
snail	....
spider	....
wasp	....
worm	....

Food from animals

cows: beef, milk	....
pigs: pork, bacon, ham, sausages	....
sheep: lamb	....
calves: veal	....
hens: chicken, eggs	....
goose: goose, eggs	....
duck: duck, eggs	....

Skin

feathers	....
wool	....
fur	....

Wild animals

alligator	....	lizard	....
bat	....	monkey	....
bear	....	panda	....
camel	....	parrot	....
cheetah	....	penguin	....
chimpanzoo	....	polar bear	....
crocodile	....	porpoise	....
deer (deer)	....	rhinoceros	....
dolphin	....	seagull	....
eagle	....	seal	....
elephant	....	shark	....
fox	....	snake	....
frog	....	squirrel	....
giraffe	....	tiger	....
gorilla	....	toad	....
hedgehog	....	tortoise	....
hippopotamus	....	whale	....
kangaroo	....	wolf (wolves)	....
leopard	....	zebra	....
lion	....		

The dolphin is my favourite wild animal
because it's very intelligent.

I don't like snakes because they're
dangerous.

I can't stand cockroaches because they're
dirty.

I'm frightened of mice because they run
so fast.

I think it's cruel to keep animals in zoos.

I think it's important to see wild animals,
even if they are in zoos.

I hate circuses with animals.

I'm in favour of hunting. You have to keep
wildlife under control.

I'm against hunting. It's cruel.

I think killing animals for meat is wrong.
I'm vegetarian.

I think you need to eat meat to keep healthy.

....
....
....
....
....
....
....
....
....
....
....
....
....
....
....

REF *See page 87 for the British / American
word list.*

1a Find the names of twenty animals in the wordsearch.

D	O	L	P	H	I	N	L	S	F
U	L	B	M	E	F	O	I	H	L
C	K	E	O	D	L	P	O	E	Y
K	P	E	N	G	U	I	N	E	G
R	A	T	K	E	B	G	O	P	O
W	C	N	E	H	S	A	F	H	O
H	R	V	Y	O	H	N	R	O	S
A	L	L	I	G	A	T	O	R	E
L	T	O	A	D	R	Y	G	S	L
E	Z	D	O	N	K	E	Y	E	B

There's not much to see here, is there?

Can we go home now, please?

1b Label the pictures using the animals from the wordsearch.

1 _dolphin_ 2 .... 3 ....

4 .... 5 .... 6 ....

7 .... 8 .... 9 ....

10 .... 11 .... 12 ....

13 .... 14 .... 15 ....

16 .... 17 .... 18 ....

19 .... 20 ....

2a Put the animals in exercise 1 into the following groups.
Add two animals to each group if you can.

mammals

....
....
....
....
....
....
....
....
....
....
....

fish

....
....
....

ANIMALS

amphibians

....
....
....
....

insects

....
....
....
....
....

birds

....
....
....
....

reptiles

....
....
....

2b Tick the animals which you can find in your country.

3 Which is the odd one out? Give a reason for your choice.

1 rat, spider, mouse, squirrel

The spider is the odd one out because it..............
is an invertebrate / has got eight legs /..............
doesn't make a noise / hasn't got fur...............

2 elephant, whale, zebra, giraffe

....
....

3 crocodile, frog, lizard, alligator

....
....

4 parrot, panda, eagle, seagull

....
....

5 leopard, tiger, wolf, lion

....
....

6 foal, chick, cow, lamb

....
....

7 fly, worm, butterfly, mosquito

....
....

4 Complete the chart.

adult	young	food
1 hen	*chick*	*chicken, eggs* ....
2 cow	....	....
3 sheep	....	....
4 duck	....	....
5 goose	....	....
6 pig	....	....

5 Try this quiz.

ANIMAL QUIZ

How much do you know about animals?

1 You find them on farms, but also in mountainous areas. They've got beards.

a) goats   b) sheep   c) bears

2 It's about 9cm long and it flies at night. It likes blood.

a) a vampire mosquito
b) a vampire parrot
c) a vampire bat

3 These animals are fish. They have teeth. Some are dangerous to people. The biggest is about 15m long.

a) whales b) sharks c) alligators

4 It lives in very cold regions. It's covered in white fur, but its skin is black.

a) a polar bear   b) a panda
c) a chimpanzee

5 It has a sort of pocket, called a 'pouch', at the front of its body, where it keeps its young.

a) a giraffe b) a kangaroo
c) a monkey

6 It lives in the sea but it isn't a fish and it isn't a reptile. It can also live out of the water. It sometimes performs in a circus.

a) a tortoise b) a porpoise   c) a seal

7 These are all types of one small animal: bird-eating, garden, gladiator, money, water, wolf and zebra.

What is the animal?

a) a rat b) a spider   c) a cockroach

8 They're invertebrates (they don't have a backbone). They move very slowly and you might find them on the menu in a restaurant in France.

a) snails   b) bees   c) wasps

9 Which is the fastest?

a) a tiger   b) a leopard   c) a cheetah

10 They haven't got legs, but they can move along the ground quickly. The biggest is 10m long and can eat large animals like deer.

a) crocodiles b) alligators c) snakes

ANSWERS
Check your answers on page G. Then read the analysis below.

ANALYSIS
9 to10 correct answers: You're going to be a vet or work on a nature reserve, right?
6 to 8 correct answers: You know your animals.
1 to 5 correct answers: Science isn't your strongest subject, is it?

6 Complete the questionnaire.

Animals and you

1 Which is your favourite wild animal? Why?   ....
2 Are there any animals you find frightening?   ....
3 If you could go anywhere in the world to study animals ...
    ● where would you go?   ....
    ● which animals would you study?   ....
4 Would you like to work with animals?   ....
5 What are your feelings about eating meat?
    ....
    ....

6 What are your feelings about horse-racing?
    ....
    ....

7 What are your feelings about zoos?
    ....
    ....

8 What are your feelings about circuses?
    ....
    ....

7 Write ten words and five expressions you are going to memorize.

Words		Expressions	
1	....	1	....
2	....		....
3	....	2	....
4	....		....
5	....	3	....
6	....		....
7	....	4	....
8	....		....
9	....	5	....
10	....		....

Test yourself 3 (Units 9 to 12)

How much can you remember?

My mark: _____
60

1 Match the phrases in column A with the phrases in column B and use them to complete the sentences.

A	B
0 I checked	a) a room at a hotel
1 I paid	b) her call
2 I spent	c) her number
3 I didn't return	d) hours on the phone last night
4 I booked	e) my e-mail
5 I sent	f) package holidays
6 I went	g) the bill
7 I called	h) the parcel first class
8 I can't stand	i) away

0 _I checked my e-mail_ .... but there were no messages for me.

9 .... next to the beach.

10 .... because I didn't have the number.

11 .... for a long weekend.

12 .... so that's why it was engaged for so long.

13 .... and left the hotel immediately.

14 .... so you should get it tomorrow.

15 .... but there was no answer.

16 .... because you have to do the same as everyone else.

(16 marks)

2 Write ...

- **the words for these landscape features**

0   _hill_ ....

1   ....

2   ....

3   ....

4   ....

5   ....

- **the phrases to describe these types of weather**

0   35°C   _It's hot._ ....

6   ....

7   ....

8   ....

9   ....

10   ....

(10 marks)

3 Complete the e-mail.

Hello from Kenya! I'm now in Mombasa, in an internet café. Cool, eh? We had a great time on 0 *safari*. We saw 1 .... , 2 .... , 3 .... and the most fabulous 4 .... There were really beautiful 5 .... in the Jadini forest. We had a picnic by a wonderful 6 .... And I rode an 7 ....! At night we sang songs around a fire and looked at the 8 .... and the 9 .... They were so bright! Of course, you had to be very careful to protect yourself from 10 .... I was a bit scared of the 11 .... , too. And one morning I found an enormous 12 .... in my shoe! We're now staying at a hotel in Mombasa for a few days. 13 .... and 14 .... of Mombasa there are fabulous 15 .... Yesterday, we went on a trip to an 16 .... just off the coast.

As usual, I've had a few disasters. The first night there was a terrible storm, with the most amazing 17 .... Our 18 .... collapsed! I got stuck in the 19 .... at the hotel this morning. And I've lost my 20 .... But apart from that, it's been great!

(20 marks)

4 Write in the missing words.

Communications
0 an internet *service* provider
1 a first-............... stamp
2 by air ....
3 directory ....
4 a touch- .... phone
5 out .... order

Weather
1 .... and lightning
2 a good .... of sunshine
3 scattered ....
4 a .... frost

Holidays
1 a .... hostel
2 pony ....
3 a caravan ....
4 a B & ....
5 room ....

(14 marks)

Reference

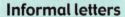

Liquid measure

See Unit 3, **Eating in and eating out**, page 18.

100 ml (millilitres) = 1 l (litre) = 1.76 pt (pints)

Informal letters

See Unit 9, **Phone, e-mail and letters**, page 59.

(number and street)   12 James Street
(town/city)   Halifax
(county)   West Yorkshire
(postcode)   HX1 2RG

(date)   5th May 20.....

Dear Rosie,
I'm glad you can come next weekend. I'm looking
forward to seeing you.
Yours / Best wishes / Love
Maria

P.S. Don't forget to bring your swimming costume!

The British postal system

First-class post should arrive the day after posting.

Second-class post should arrive by the third working day after posting.

Special delivery is for valuable items which need to arrive before twelve o'clock (midday) the day after posting.

Recorded delivery is for important (but not valuable) items which can go either first or second class.

The definite article with geographical names

See Unit 11, **Landscape and weather**, page 70.

Use the definite article with names of

oceans	the Atlantic, the Indian Ocean
seas	the Mediterranean, the Baltic
rivers	the Danube, the Mississippi
mountain ranges	the Alps, the Andes
groups of islands	the Seychelles, the West Indies
deserts	the Sahara, the Gobi Desert

Do not use the definite article with names of

individual mountains	Mount Everest, Mount Kilimanjaro
volcanoes	Etna, Vesuvius
islands	Jamaica, Sardinia
lakes	Lake Michigan, Lake Balaton

Temperature

See Unit 11, **Landscape and weather**, page 71.

Celsius (Centigrade)
$$°C = (°F - 32) \times \frac{5}{9}$$

Fahrenheit
$$°F = \frac{9 \times °C}{5} + 32$$

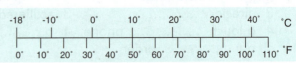

Some basic spelling rules

REF See also **Boost Your Vocabulary 1**, page 85, for Some basic spelling rules.

Adjectives: comparatives and superlatives

1. To make the comparative and superlative of regular one-syllable and some two-syllable adjectives: add -er and -est

	comparative	superlative
long	longer	longest

2. Adjectives which end in -e: add -r and -st for the comparative and superlative

	comparative	superlative
wide	wider	widest

3. Adjectives which end in -y

-y ⟹	comparative -ier ⟹	superlative -iest
early	earlier	earliest
heavy	heavier	heaviest

4. One-syllable adjectives which end in a single consonant: double the consonant before adding -er or -est

	comparative	superlative
big	bigger	biggest
hot	hotter	hottest
wet	wetter	wettest

5. When the vowel which comes before the final consonant is not stressed, or when it is spelled with two letters: do not double the consonant

	comparative	superlative
quiet	quieter	quietest
great	greater	greatest

6. Do not double y or w at the end of words

new	newer	newest

Adjectives and adverbs

1. To make an adjective into an adverb: add -ly

adjective	adverb
nice	nicely
quiet	quietly

2. Adjectives which end in -y

adjective	adverb
-y ⟹	-ily
noisy	noisily
easy	easily

3. Adjectives which end in -le: drop the e before adding -ly

adjective	adverb
simple	simply
terrible '	terribly

REF See **Boost Your Vocabulary 3**, for the comparatives and superlatives of two-syllable adjectives.

British / American spellings

British	American	
litre	liter	(See page 18.)
burnt	burned	(See page 19.)
theatre	theater	(See page 24.)
(health) centre	(health) center	(See page 24.)
jeweller's	jeweler's	(See page 25.)
programme	program	(See page 39.)
colour	color	(See page 39.)
cheque	check	(See page 44.)
travellers' cheques	travelers' checks	(See pages 44 and 64.)

British and American English

British	American
1 Physical description *(See page 6.)*	
spots	pimples
a fringe	bangs
in bunches	in ponytails
in plaits	in braids / pigtails
2 House and home *(See page 12.)*	
cooker	stove
hob	range / cooktop
fridge	refrigerator
taps	faucets
bin	trash can
work surface	counter
standard lamp	floor lamp
toilet roll	toilet paper
towel rail	towel rack
washbasin	sink
linen basket	clothes basket
flannel	washcloth
chest of drawers	dresser
notice board	bulletin board
radio alarm	clock radio
wardrobe	closet *(built-in type)*
detached house	single-family house
semi-detached house	duplex/two-family house
terraced house	row house
bungalow	ranch house
flat	apartment
in + *name of street*	on + *name of street*
city centre	downtown
opposite	across from
whereabouts	where
3 Eating in and eating out *(See page 18.)*	
packet (of crisps)	bag (of potato chips)
tub (of ice-cream)	carton (of ice-cream)
tin	can
grill	broil
side plate	salad plate
jug	pitcher
table mat	place mat
takeaway	takeout
starter	appetizer
bill	check
horrible	awful / terrible
chips	French fries
lemonade	lemon-lime drink
jam	jam, *also* jelly
underdone	undercooked
4 Places in towns *(See page 24.)*	
railway station	train station
sports centre	the gym / health club

British	American
university	college (*in formal language,* university *may be used*)
cinema	movie theater
games arcade	arcade
disco	club
laundrette	laundromat
doctor's surgery	doctor's office
estate agent's	real estate office
bookshop	book store
greengrocer's	fruit and vegetable market
fishmonger's	fish market
chemist's	drug store / pharmacy
newsagent's	news dealer / news stand
off licence	liquor store
hairdresser's	beauty shop
(record / toy) shop	(record / toy) store
electrical goods store	electrical supply store
clothes shop	clothing store
corner shop	convenience store
market	farmer's market
has got a sale on	is having a sale
Are you being served?	May I help you?
It's on special offer.	It's on sale.
You've got toothache.	You have a toothache.
on holiday	on vacation
a lettuce	a head of lettuce
5 Travel and transport *(See page 32.)*	
coach	bus
tram	streetcar / trolley
lorry	truck
motorbike	motorcycle
scooter	moped
transport	transportation / transit
underground	subway
left-luggage (office)	baggage room
toilets:	restroom:
gentlemen / gents	men's room
ladies	women's / powder room
refreshments	snack bar
timetable	schedule
standard class (second class)	second class
non-smoking compartment	no-smoking car
buffet car	dining car
sleeper	sleeper / sleeping car

British	American
single (ticket)	one-way (ticket)
return (ticket)	round-trip (ticket)
rail card	pass / farecard
queue (*noun*)	line
baggage reclaim	baggage claim
hand luggage	carry-on bag
ticket collector	conductor
cabin attendant	flight attendant
to book	to reserve
way out	exit

6 Cinema, television and radio (See page 38.)

British	American
current affairs programme	current events program
chat show / talk show	talk show
comedy series	variety show
Roxy Cinema	Roxy Theater
film	movie
bit	part
adverts	commercials

7 Money (See page 44.)

British	American
purse	coin purse / change purse
cashier	teller
enquiries	customer service desk
current account	checking account
cheque book	check book
paying-in book	deposit slips
pocket money / spending money	allowance
helping on a market stall	helping at / in a market
till	cash register / checkout counter
mean	cheap / stingy
careful with money	thrifty
careless with money	a spendthrift

8 Personal belongings, clothes and shoes
(See page 50.)

British	American
rucksack	backpack / daypack
mobile phone	cell(ular) phone
diary	date book / organizer
brooch	pin
hair slide	barrette
trainers	running shoes / sneakers
flat shoes	flats
lace-ups	Oxfords
slip-ons	loafers
plimsolls	sneakers
spotted	polka-dot
zip	zipper

British	American
jumper	sweater / pullover sweater

9 Phone, e-mail and letters (See page 58.)

British	American
phone box	phone booth
handset	receiver
directory enquiries	information / directory assistance
to ring someone	to call someone
to put the phone down (on someone)	to hang up (on someone)
It's engaged.	It's busy.
postcode	zip code
post box	mailbox / drop box
postman / postwoman	mail carrier
post	mail

10 Holidays (See page 64.)

British	American
holiday	vacation
countryside	country
package holiday	package tour
walking	hiking
caravan site	trailer park
full board	American plan
lift	elevator
first floor	second floor
Could I put it on my room?	Please charge it to my room.
caravan	trailer
pitch (*space for a tent*)	tent site
play area	playground
mini-golf / crazy golf	miniature golf
pony trekking	pack trip
cycle hire	bicycle rental
to hire	to rent

11 Landscape and weather (See page 70.)

British	American
a good deal of sunshine.	mostly sunny
sunny periods	partly sunny
midday	noon

12 The animal world (See page 76.)

no entries for this section

Bye!

USA

Self assessment and progress check

Self assessment

Fill in the chart when you have completed each unit.

	Which vocabulary sections were the most useful? (e.g. Hair style)	How well did you do in the exercises? very | quite | not so well Tick the correct part of the line.	You wrote down some words and expressions to memorize. How many of them can you remember? Words /10 Expressions /5	Which vocabulary sections do you need to go over again before you do the test?
1 Physical description				
2 House and home				
3 Eating in and eating out				
4 Places in towns				

Test score: / 60

5 Travel and transport				
6 Cinema, television and radio				
7 Money				
8 Personal belongings, clothes and shoes				

Test score: / 60

9 Phone, e-mail and letters				
10 Holidays				
11 Landscape and weather				
12 The animal world				

Test score: / 60

Progress check

How much of the vocabulary did you know **before** you worked through the units?
How much do you feel you know **after** working through the units?

		Less than 25%	About 50%	More than 60%
Units 1 – 4	before			
	after			
Units 5 – 8	before			
	after			
Units 9 – 12	before			
	after			